SAFE
From
Terrorism

How To Protect and Save
Yourself and Your Family
At Home, Work, and Play

Michael E. Bemis

Hanrow
Press h·p

Ta...

Introduction

The tragic events that unfolded before our eyes on the morning of September 11, 2001 shall never fully fade from memory. Those incidents, coupled with the disturbing events of the 1990's, the so-called disaster decade, have altered the American psyche. As we look forward at this difficult time in history, we try to make sense of this brutal enemy that is both distant and disturbingly close. We grapple with the reality that the United States is the target of choice, and the realization that this threat rivals the peril of communism and socialism.

The recent domestic enemies of our past weren't so elusive. There were many opportunities to aid in the crusade against crime, drunk driving, and substance abuse. However, there is little we can do collectively about the terrorism that has stained our homeland, except support our government's efforts to eradicate this evil.

Therefore, our efforts to make tomorrow better are focused solely on ways to keep our families and ourselves safe. Safe From Terrorism, partially written before 9/11, is packed with practical, do-it-yourself advice.

To fully protect yourself from terrorism, you will have many things to do. Everything you do will make you safer and make you feel safer. You may choose not to do some of which is contained in Safe From Terrorism. However, remember that these are life and death issues. The things you don't do make you vulnerable.

Safe From Terrorism focuses on prevention. That is, things that you can do to stay clear of terrorism. While the book contains defensive strategies, the emphasis is on what to do from an offensive standpoint. Defense assumes you'll be coming face to face with terrorism. Is that what you want? Of course not! Safe From Terrorism seeks to ensure that you stay out of harm's way, not be armed to take it head on and survive the aftermath.

Terrorism preparation that is motivated by a single event, particularly unprecedented ones like those that took place on 9/11, is not good. You must anticipate and be prepared for other types of terrorist attacks. Your terrorism preparation should be like your 401k—highly diversified.

Whatever you chose to do to protect your family and yourself from terrorism, make sure you sustain it. Don't let your response to what's happened be a flash in the plan, a knee jerk reaction. While we will never forget the horrific events of 9/11, we are destined to forget most of what we thought was so right immediately following that dreadful day.

People will eventually expect and in some cases demand that the level of government security imposed after the attacks be reduced or eliminated. This will be especially true with those measures that are invasive, slow, and unsightly. Even though most of these security measures are sensible, some probably won't be sustained by a freedom loving country like America.

However, the opposite is also true. The endless flow of recommendations that preceded the Y2K scare is a case in point. The suggestion that you should have built a concrete basement bunker and stocked it to the roof with survival equipment and supplies was ridiculous. These feel good measures don't endure because they're not sensible. Some of them are simply the result of savvy merchandisers seeking greater profits.

The contents of *Safe From Terrorism* are reasoned and reasonable; this allows you to achieve a level of safety from terrorism that is not only protective but also sustainable.

Staying safe is a daily, lifetime endeavor. Like eating right, exercising regularly, and saving for retirement, staying safe requires an enduring commitment from you.

When it comes to terrorism, you are not a target. Unlike identification theft, harassment, pick pocketing, burglary, and rape, terrorists aren't interested in you specifically. In fact, terrorists don't even know you. They don't know John or Mary Smith.

You are not a target because terrorists don't seek personal gain. They don't have personal needs. They don't have an ax to grind with you. Their brand of victimization is wholesale terror. That's not to say you won't be *one* of their victims, but it's highly unlikely you'll be targeted. Unless you are a high-ranking politician or government official, a prominent corporate leader, or celebrity with a household name, you likely won't be singled out.

However, the effectiveness of terrorism is dependent on garnering national and international media attention. The most effective acts of terrorism involve the killing and/or maiming of every day people. While becoming a victim of terrorism can be dependent on whom you are, we must remember that none of the people killed on 9/11 were famous or classifiable in any group other than being Americans.

Chapter 1

Your Are Not A Target

When it comes to terrorism, you are not a target. Unlike identification theft, harassment, pick pocketing, burglary, and rape, terrorists aren't interested in you specifically. In fact, terrorists don't even know you. They don't know John or Mary Smith.

You are not a target because terrorists don't seek personal gain. They don't have personal needs. They don't have an ax to grind with you. Their brand of victimization is wholesale terror. That's not to say you won't be one of their victims, but it's highly unlikely you'll be targeted. Unless you are a high-ranking politician or government official, a prominent corporate leader, or celebrity with a household name, you likely won't be singled out.

However, the effectiveness of terrorism is dependent on garnering national and international media attention. The most effective acts of terrorism involve the killing and/or maiming of every day people. While becoming a victim of terrorism can be dependent on whom you are, we must remember that none of the people killed on 9/11 were famous or classifiable in any group other than being Americans.

Chapter 2

The Preventative Advantage

You want to be safe from terrorism. Therefore your immediate reaction might be to purchase or partake of everything being advertised as being anti-terrorist.

However, personal protection equipment, supplies, and training assume you'll be confronting terrorism head-on. Is that what you want? Of course not!

The key to staying safe is to stay out of harm's way. It is far better to know how to avoid completely an encounter with a terrorist than it is to have the tools and skills to foil his face-to-face attempt to injury or kill you.

Safe From Terrorism seeks to ensure that you stay out of danger by offering a variety of pre-emptive measures.

Chapter 3

Making Prudent Safety Decisions

Making prudent safety decisions should not be an activity that you indulge in only following an act of terrorism. On the contrary, safety decisions should meet or exceed the following criteria:

- They should be made and reassessed daily.

- They should not necessarily be what government officials are recommending.

- They should be influenced by external events.

- They should never be influenced by the passage of time.

- They should never be influenced by financial constraints.

- They should never be influenced by culture, religion, or ideology.

- They should never be influenced by the opinions of family, friends, and colleagues.

Chapter 4

Widespread Applicability

If you follow any or all of the advice in *Safe From Terrorism* you'll be safer and you'll feel safer. In addition, that level of safety won't be limited to acts of terrorism. This is the case because the advice isn't proprietary. Much of it has widespread, lifetime applicability.

Much of what *Safe From Terrorism* contains makes sense even absent the events of 9/11. In fact, some of the book was researched and written before that tragic day.

The survival suggestions are applicable to most any disaster. When you are prepared for terrorism and it's aftermath, you are equally prepared for the eventuality of blizzards, earthquakes, floods, hurricanes, tornados, and wildfires.

When you avoid known terrorist targets, you are also avoiding a host of accidental dangers. For example, if you choose to avoid living near a nuclear power reactor, a potential terrorism target, you will also be avoiding the possibility of an accident at the plant.

By avoiding many known terrorist targets, you will also be protecting your home ownership investment. Having known terrorist targets nearby is never desirable.

Chapter 5
Preventing The Preventable

There are things in life that can be prevented. There are things in life that can't. The things that can be prevented are preventable when we take reasonable safety measures. The things that can't be prevented are so because we rightly refuse to live our lives in a bubble.

From a safety standpoint, it is important to have the knowledge to make the distinction between what we should do and what we shouldn't do to protect our family and ourselves. This is especially true when it come to the insidious and ever-present threat of terrorism.

For example, roadways are dangerous places. When you operate a motor vehicle down a public way, you are placing your family and yourself at risk. While there is no way to remove the risks completely, the degree of danger is to a great extent within your control. Look at the list of controllable risk factors for motor vehicles in Chapter 29. If all of them are in your favor you've done all you can. You've prevented the preventable. The rest is fate.

The same is true of terrorism. The wealth of advice contained in this book aids you in preventing the preventable. By preventing the preventable, you will greatly decrease the probability of being a victim of an act of terrorism. You will go forth secure in the knowledge that you have left no stone unturned in your quest to keep your family and yourself safe.

Chapter 6

Staying Informed

There is widespread agreement that the most effective way to fight terrorism is with intelligence. While you can't have the agents, networks, sources, and resources that the government has, you none-the-less can do your own intelligence gathering and analyzing.

How? By listening to radio news, watching television news, reading newspapers and magazines, and visiting Internet World Wide Web news sites. From these sources, you will learn the threats, the trends, the methods, and most importantly, the precautions you need to be taking.

You may tire of the news. However, staying tuned is a vital part of staying safe. If you are not privy to what's going on, you can't protect your family and yourself. Forewarned is forearmed.

Consider doing the following:

- At the very least, partake of live or regularly up-dated broad cast news at meal times. In a traditional day that means early morning, around noon, and evening. In a non-traditional day, it could be mid-morning, late afternoon, and around midnight. Using several mediums and sources is best to get a well-round ed picture.

- Read at least one print publication every day, preferably a regional or national newspaper. Print publications are an essential supplement to broadcast news. They provide far more than the headlines. The depth and variety of their news goes far beyond what broadcast sources can and do provide.

Beyond The Headlines

While the daily news is vital, it is equally important to delve into matters a little deeper once a week. A news magazine scanned or read cover to cover will do nicely. In addition, the Internet's World Wide Web offers a diverse number of content sites that provide interesting angles and analysis on a number of timely subjects.

Talk To Others

Talk frequently and openly with others. What's their opinion of what happened or what's happening? What precautions are they taking? Your conversations with them will probably provide you with their state of mind. Taken collectively, the mental state of those you talk to can provide valuable insight. The more people who are in tune with anti-terrorism preparation, the less likely they will be targets. Terrorists rely on predictable human behavior. Their "success" depends on the unexpected. They do not want to be in unpredictable situations or having to deal with highly prepared people.

Chapter 7

Who You Are Counts

The most deadly occupations in the United States are found in outdoor occupations or jobs where workers are not in an office or factory. These include truck drivers, farmers, construction laborers, and airplane pilots. Other jobs that are dangerous include commercial fishing, timber cutters, retail store clerks, and taxicab drivers.

However, when it comes to terrorism, it is different. Occupations or jobs where workers are in an office or factory create greater risk.

Generally, you are at greater risk if one or more of the following apply:

- You are employed by a government or quasi-government agency, especially those at the federal level.

- You hold an important appointed or elected government position, especially if it is a visible leadership job.

- You are a member of the military.

- You are a public safety worker.

- You are a provider of direct health care.

- You are a member of the media, especially the national media, and you are in a high profile position.

- You work for an organization that engages in a controversial special interest.

- You work in or near a likely terrorist target.

Chapter 8

Where You Are
Location, Location, Location

While acts of terrorism are highly unpredictable events, your location is the single greatest factor in your risk of attack.

Location is most important when it comes to your home. While it is highly unlikely terrorists will strike your home, their targets can directly and indirectly affect you where you live if you are not careful.

In addition to where your home is situated, location also refers to the following:

• The site of your business.

• Where you work.

• Where you go to school.

• Where you go to summer camp.

• Where you partake of entertainment.

• Where you vacation.

• The destinations of your business trips.

• Your routes of travel.

This chapter will deal exclusively with location. More specifically, it will address the three components of location: **place, position,** and **proximity.**

Place

First, there is the place where you are. Generally, place relates to your location every moment of everyday. Place includes all the countries and regions of the world. It includes all locations in the United States including regions and states. It also includes those areas in the United States classified as urban, suburban, and rural.

Historical Perspective

The greatest predictor of the future is the past. While not foolproof, such an assertion does have merit. It is for that reason that we should look closely at the past to guide our choices for the future. A detailed look at both international and domestic terrorism during the past two decades as it relates to place-s is necessary.

International Terrorism

The U. S. Department of State - Office of the Coordinator for Counterterrorism defines International terrorism as follows:

The term "international terrorism" means terrorism involving citi - zens or the territory of more than one country.

There is no question that by residing in North America, you are significantly safer from international terrorism than anywhere else in the world. For example, according to *Patterns of Global Terrorism 2000*, released by the *U. S. Department of State - Office of the Coordinator for Counterterrorism* in April 2001, there were a mere 15 international terrorism attacks from 1995-2000 in North America. In contrast, Latin America and Western Europe experienced 729 and 608 international terrorism attacks from 1995-2000 respectively.

Being An Expatriate

Many large companies offer their employees the chance to be an expatriate—a person who is voluntarily living and working abroad. While being an expatriate in some countries would seem wonderful, doing it anywhere is no longer a good idea. Even if the coun-try where you will be living and working seems a safe one, being an expatriate has a variety of dangers associated with it. Consider the following:

Expatriates travel more in a year than most people do in a lifetime. Increased travel equates to higher risk.

As an American, you could become the target of anti-American sentiment. The possibility of terrorist acts aimed at U. S. citizens and interest abroad has always been a concern and was exacerbated following the events of 9/11.

If domestic or international affairs become unstable, you could be forced to evacuate the country where you live and work or you could become stranded or detained in that country, possibly for a long period.

Domestic Terrorism

The Federal Bureau of Investigation (FBI) defines domestic terrorism as follows:

Domestic terrorism is the unlawful use, or threatened use, of force or violence by a group or individual based and operating entirely within the United States or its territories without foreign direction committed against persons or property to intimidate or coerce a government, the civilian population, or any segment thereof, in furtherance of political or social objectives.

According to *Terrorism in the United States* 1999, between 1980-1999, the *Federal Bureau of Investigation (FBI)* recorded 457 terrorist incidents, suspected terrorist incidents, and preventions in the United States.

Terrorist incidents, suspected terrorist incidents, and preventions are defined as follows:

- *A terrorist incident is a violent act or an act dangerous to human life, in violation of the criminal laws of the United States, or of any state, to intimidate or coerce a government, the civilian population, or any segment thereof, in furtherance of political or social objectives.*

- *A suspected terrorist incident is a potential act of terrorism for which responsibility cannot be attributed to a known or suspected group. Assessment of the circumstances surrounding the act determines its inclusion in this category.*

- *A terrorism prevention is a documented example in which a violent act by a known or suspected terrorist group or individual with the means and a proven propensity for violence is successfully interdicted through investigative activity.*

Regions

Regionally, the Northeastern United States had the greatest number of terrorist incidents, suspected terrorist incidents, and preventions (140). The North Central region of the United States had the fewest (52).

Looking at this data as presented can be misleading. If we reduce the larger regions into smaller ones the picture is much different. For example, the Northeastern region had the most incidents. New England is a part of the Northeastern region. However, New England had only four terrorist incidents, suspected terrorist incidents, and preventions during the two-decade period—three in Massachusetts and one in Vermont.

Narrowing the region even further, northern New England, which consists of New Hampshire, Maine, and Vermont, only had one recorded incident during the two decades, which is classified as an attempted bombing, or prevention.

Needless to say, Puerto Rico, given its size, is infested with terrorism. Puerto Rico is only 3,435 square miles, which is a fraction of one percent of the size of the United States. However, 22.5 percent of all recorded terrorist incidents, suspected terrorist incidents, and preventions occurred there.

States

A detailed analysis of terrorist incidents, suspected terrorist incidents, and preventions contained in Terrorism in the United States 1999 shows distinct geographical concentrations of terrorism. For example, specific terrorism incident data for 1990-1999 shows the location of 43 terrorist attacks in the United States. These 43 terrorist attacks occurred in only 14 states.

This means that no known terrorist activity occurred in the other 36 states during the 1990's.

Data for the period 1980-1989 lists 307 terrorist incidents, suspected terrorist incidents, and preventions in the United States. Removing the 81 that occurred in Puerto Rico leaves 226 that took place in the 50 states of the United States.

These events occurred in only 27 states as follows:

State	Number
New York	73
Florida	34
California	27
Washington D.C.	16
Maryland	14

Illinois	**9**
Idaho	**9**
Arizona	**6**
Michigan	**6**
New Jersey	**5**
Louisiana	**4**
Kansas	**3**
Massachusetts	**3**
Colorado	**2**
Montana	**2**
Texas	**2**
Hawaii	**1**
Minnesota	**1**
Missouri	**1**
North Dakota	**1**
Ohio	**1**
Oklahoma	**1**
Oregon	**1**
Pennsylvania	**1**
Tennessee	**1**
Virginia	**1**
Vermont	**1**

This means that no known terrorist activity occurred in the other 23 states during the 1980's.

State Correlations

Not surprisingly, terrorist incidents, suspected terrorist incidents, and preventions in the United States correlate to population and targets.

The four most populous states according to Census 2000 conducted by the U. S. Census Bureau are also three of the top terrorism states— New York, Florida, and California.

Washington D. C. and Maryland, both of which have relatively small populations, rank fourth and fifth in terrorism. The number of desirable terrorist targets they contain accounts for this deviation.

Passing Through States

Terrorists may pass through and even linger in the so-called terrorism free states. They may procure money, equipment, or supplies in them. They might finalize plans. However, there is a very good chance that they would not subject these states to their wrath. Their goal is to strike their intended target. The one that fits the bill. This means they will be on their best behavior before the act because they won't want to jeopardize their mission.

Urban, Suburban, Or Rural?

Where would you be safer from terrorism? In the wilderness of Northern Maine or in the concrete jungle that is lower Manhattan. Few people would argue that the answer is the former.

Urban areas are more likely to be affected directly or indirectly by terrorism than those located elsewhere. This is because they contain many likely terrorist targets and because they're population centers.

In fact, an analysis of terrorist incidents, suspected terrorist incidents, and preventions in the United States from 1980-1999 revealed the following:

• Of the 76 incidents that occurred in the state of New York, 83 percent occurred in New York City.

• Of the 34 incidents that occurred in the state of Florida, 88 percent occurred in Miami.

Urban, Suburban, Or Rural?

Where would you be safer from terrorism? In the wilderness of Northern Maine or in the concrete jungle that is lower Manhattan. Few people would argue that the answer is the former.

Urban areas are more likely to be affected directly or indirectly by terrorism than those located elsewhere. This is because they contain many likely terrorist targets and because they're population centers.

This means that during this period, 36 percent, well over one third, of all recorded incidents occurred on just three-thousandths of the landmass of the United States.

Therefore, it is not wise to paint with the same color brush the states listed as having the most terrorist incidents, suspected terrorist incidents, and preventions.

What you should do is to determine population density, or persons per square mile. This is accomplished easily by visiting the U. S. Census Bureau World Wide Web site on the Internet at the following address. www.census.gov

When you reach the site, go to the American FactFinder and look up persons per square mile for your state. Using shaded areas, you will be able to determine in a minute or so where the population is concentrated relative to the rest of the state. You can also elect to add features like the location of airports and military installations.

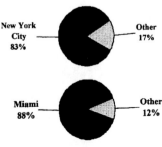

While the terrorism threat diminishes proportionately to the miles away from urban areas, it is not recommended that you choose a home in a rural area. While the terrorism threat is probably at its lowest in rural areas, there are a variety of other factors, all of which outweigh the small-added benefit of being in the middle of nowhere. What's best? Overall, homes in suburban areas offer the best protection.

Suburban Is Best

The best place to live from all standpoints, including terrorism, is suburbia, especially fringe suburban. Fringe suburbia refers to suburban areas that are close to rural areas. Fringe suburban areas can often be identified using the following criteria:

• They are often located from 25 to 50 miles from urban areas.

• Their population range is often from approximately 5,000 to 15,000.

• There is likely no or limited public mass transportation.

• The tallest buildings are no more than several floors.

• There is no appreciable difference between their daytime and nighttime population.

• They may be referred to as "bedroom towns."

Position

The second most important factor is your position within a given place. Where you live. Where you work. The location where you shop and partake of services. The location of your pastimes. The location where you go for leisure.

If you are in a safe place, your position within that place doesn't really matter because the entire place is relatively safe provided there are no known terrorist targets located in the area. In contrast, if you are in an urban area, your position is vital to the degree of safety that exists because the entire place is relatively unsafe.

Proximity

The third factor is proximity, that is, how close you are to known or likely terrorist targets.

Terrorists historically strike targets that will injure or maim the most people, do the most direct damage, inflict the greatest collateral damage, disrupt services to the greatest number of consumers, or inflict the greatest economic hardship.

They also favor those that represent symbolism, those that are likely to leave people stricken with fear or grief, and those that will elicit the greatest degree of national and international media attention.

Target Identification

According to the Federal Bureau of Investigation (FBI), terrorist targets generally fall into five broad categories, some of which overlap, depending on the motives of those planning the attack. These categories are as follows:

- **Symbolic or public message targets** - These are the most common and by far the largest category. They include prominent landmarks, electrical utilities, pipelines, state and local government buildings, universities, certain federal government buildings, and/or businesses and industries involved in such areas as chemical production, animal research, forest or wood products, and refineries.

- **Government-owned or -operated facilities** - These consist of tunnels, computer facilities, airports, state capitols, bridges and overpasses, maritime facilities (e.g. locks and harbors), and law enforcement buildings and support structures.

- **Military targets** - (e.g. military bases, museums, and testing facilities). While generally more secure that other potential tar gets, these offer an immense opportunity to embarrass the mili tary and the U. S. government.

- **Cybertargets** - These include the computer-operated control systems and networks for utilities, utility distribution, air traffic control centers, financial networks, emergency 9-1-1 systems, and other vital services that rely on computer-operated control systems and networks.

- **Individual victims** - This category includes assassinations, extortions, and the kidnapping of appointed and elected gov ernment officials.

These targets are generally easy to identify and avoid. Make sure your home is located at least a mile, and preferably many miles, from these terrorist targets.

The following is a more detailed list of named terrorist targets. Those that are marked with an asterisk may be of less concern. For example, a local airport that handles only private aircraft is of less concern than a large urban airport that handles commercial flights. Likewise, a municipal or county government complex is of less concern than a state or federal government complex.

- Chemical Production Plants

- Computer Infrastructure

- Electrical Power
    Distribution Facilities
    Hydroelectric Dams
    Generation Plants
    Transmission Lines

- Financial Institutions*

- Fuel
  - Oil Rigs
  - Refineries
  - Tank Farms
  - Natural Gas
  - Petroleum

- Government Complexes*

- Historic Sites*

- Military Facilities

- National Monuments

- Public Water Supplies
  - Dams
  - Pumping Stations
  - Reservoirs

- Aerospace Facilities

- Telecommunications
  - Facilities
  - Infrastructure
  - Towers

- Transportation
  - Airports*
  - Bridges*
  - Harbors*
  - Railways*
  - Seaports*
  - Subways*
  - Terminals*
  - Tunnels*

- Tourist Attractions*

- Universities*

Targets That Are Unique

Places that are unique—one-of-a-kind—are often targets. Anything that can carry the label as being the largest, tallest, longest, deepest, oldest, newest, or safest could be a target.

The World Trade Center (WTC), twice a terrorist target, was certainly an icon. At 110 stories, it dominated parts of the New York City skyline. It represented corporate America and capitalism as few structures did.

National historical sites, such as a national monument, like the Statue of Liberty, are certainly unique, high profile structures.

Other unique targets include those that are engaged in something unique, for example, a university has a unique national or international program that is on the leading edge of technology, science, or some other discipline, especially if it is controversial.

Targets That Are Controversial

Targets that are controversial are often related to special interest terrorism. Special interest terrorism consists of extremist groups who attempt to influence specific issues rather than widespread political change. These issues include the following:

• Animal rights

• Anti-nuclear

• Environmental

• Pro-life

Targets That Are Vital

A tunnel or bridge that is the only link between two places is a vital target, especially if it is a heavily traveled commuter route.

Other vital targets include power generating facilities, power distribution systems, and telecommunications infrastructure. This is especially the case when they serve a large population.

Targets With Secondary Impact

Targets with secondary impact are attractive to terrorists because they reap the most for their efforts. For example, consider the destruction of a large hydroelectric dam. The direct impact—the destruction of the dam—could be significant in itself. Lives could be lost. The cost of rebuilding the dam could be significant both in terms of cost and the number of years it would take to rebuild.

However, enormous secondary impact could result as follows:

- The loss of possibly crucial electrical generation capacity.

- The possibility of widespread lowland flooding. This could result in many deaths and the widespread destruction of property.

The secondary impact of an attack on a nuclear power plant could come in the form of radiation exposure to possibly thousands of people and widespread contamination, the effects of which could last for minimally decades.

Fame and Fortune Targets

Do not attempt to be or live near celebrities. They are choice terrorism targets.

Avoiding Targets

With a little thought and research, you can easily avoid known terrorist targets or those your family or you fear most.

For instance, suppose you want to avoid nuclear power reactors because they're a known terrorist target or because the thought of one of them being attacked sends shivers up your spine.

According to the Nuclear Regulatory Commission, there are 104 commercial nuclear power reactors—those that generate electricity—in the United States. They are located in just 31 states. There are also 36 non-power reactors located primarily at universities where they are used for research, testing, and training.

Clearly, if the nuclear power reactor threat concerns you, you should consider living in the Midwest. There is a large area of the country, representing many states, which is free of nuclear power reactors.

For instance, is you choose to live in the southwest corner of Wyoming, say Rock Springs, you'll be about 500 miles as the crow flies from the nearest nuclear power reactor. There are a few non-power reactor sites in the area.

If you want to be even further from nuclear power reactors, consider living in Alaska or Hawaii, where there are no power or non-power nuclear reactor sites.

Also, consider the following facts:

• Over 80 percent of the nuclear power reactors in the United States are located on or east of the Mississippi River.

• The worst place for nuclear sites is the east cost where the con centration of nuclear power reactors is very high.

• The worst state is Illinois, where there are 14 nuclear power reactors, followed by Pennsylvania where there are 10.

This nuclear power reactor information was complied with little effort. So if a particular type of terrorist threat troubles you, don't let it get you down. Determine where the threat doesn't exist, or where it's minor in nature, or where it might be mitigated by prevailing conditions, and act accordingly. In some cases, the information alone could allay your fears.

Chapter 9

The Changing Face of Terrorism
Shifting The Threat

For many actions that are taken, there is a reaction. Terrorism is no different. This means that the terrorist targets of the past may not necessarily be the ones of the future. Over the past decade, many likely terrorist targets in the United States were subjected to increased security. Following the terrorist attacks of 9/11 an unprecedented wave of security improvements has taken place.

Here are some examples:

- Following the April 19, 1995 bombing of the *Alfred P. Murrah Federal Building* in Oklahoma City, Oklahoma, many government facilities, especially federal ones, were fortified. This makes the possibility of a successful terrorist attack less likely. Following the attack on the Pentagon on 9/11 and the possibility that another federal government facility was being targeted, security at federal government facilities has been strengthened.

- Following the February 26, 1993 act of terrorism at the *World Trade Center (WTC)* and the most recent one on 9/11, security at corporate sites has been in some cases established and in others strengthened.

- Airport security, especially at airports that handle commercial air traffic, has undergone sweeping security improvements fol lowing 9/11. This will make future terrorist acts at airports very difficult. The level of security implemented is not likely to be lowered or eliminated.

Chapter 10
New Methods
Weapons of Mass Destruction (WMD)

Weapons of Mass Destruction (WMD) have not been widely employed by terrorists. From 1980-1999, there were only five recorded incidents. However, their use poses a chilling and serious threat.

Chemical, Biological, and Radiological

According to the *Federal Bureau of Investigation (FBI)*, the procurement and use of chemical, biological, and radiological materials with the intent to harm have shown a steady increase since 1995. Most cases have involved hoaxes rather than actual use.

A terrorist attack involving chemical, biological, or radiological materials presents the greatest danger. Consider the following:

- The incident might not be recognizable until there were multi ple casualties or there may be more than one incident.

- Contamination could spread quickly. It might not be possible to contain it.

- Public safety and health workers could easily be contaminated as could vital facilities and even mutual aid jurisdictions.

- The public reaction will be far greater than with any other type of incident. Panic could easily ensue.

A terrorist attack involving chemical, biological, or radiological materials would likely be unleashed in an urban area in order to maximize its potential.

Agroterrorism

The attack on agriculture, livestock, or other food supplies using chemical, biological, and radiological materials is known as agroterrorism.

Cyberterrorism

Cyberterrorism is electronic, information-based terrorism which comes in two forms. First, computers and the Internet are used by terrorists to securely communicate for a variety of purposes. Second, cyber-based attacks can be used to inflict crippling damage on critical electronic systems.

Sound and Electromagnetism

High Energy Radio Frequency (HERF) and Electromagnetic Pulse (EMP) are weapons that can overload, damage, or destroy electronic systems.

New Precautions

So how do you protect yourself from Weapons of Mass Destruction? The most effective method would be if you could live, should the need arise, just as your ancestors did. While chemical, biological, and radiological attacks could still be problematic, you would be far better off than most.

Agroterrorism, Cyberterrorism, and High Energy Radio Frequency (HERF) and Electromagnetic Pulse (EMP) attacks would likely be nonevents in your household because you would be self sufficient in terms of water and food supplies and you would not be dependent on anything electronic.

The very notion of being able to do this in an urban area is absurd. In a suburban area, it would be highly difficult. In a rural area, it would probably be possible.

However, living in a rural area to ward off the minuscule threat that exists from Weapons of Mass Destruction is heavily outweighed by the other disadvantages you face when you reside in such a place, in addition to the hardship and inconvenience you would endure.

Therefore, the recommendation in the "Location, Location, Location" section of this book should prevail. The best place for your primary residence is suburban, especially fringe suburban. The recommendation in the "Alternative Safe Havens" section of this book should also prevail. The best place for your alternative safe haven is in a rural area.

Chapter 11

Home
Your Safe Haven

Of all the things you do to safeguard yourself from terrorism, your home should be the priority. Here is why:

• Nowhere is it more important for your family and you to be safe than at home.

• Your family and you likely spend more time at home than anywhere.

• Following an act of terrorism and the social disorder that could follow, you will want to be home. In the case of a declared state of emergency or the implementation of martial law, you will be required to go home and stay there. This could be for an extended period.

• When you are at home, you are the least dependent on other people for the safety of your family and yourself.

• Home is likely the only place where you can exercise total control. Therefore, it is the only place you can be completely safe.

• Because you exercise total control of your home, it is probably the only place you can make completely self-sufficient.

• Because you own or have ownership rights in your home, you have the rights that go with it. Your home is sovereign territory. Among other things, the United States Constitution provides sacred protection for the home against unreasonable searches and seizures.

• If you or another person is not in imminent danger, you may not have the right to defend your home. However, the law would likely look most favorably upon an act of protecting property if it was your home that was being defended.

Chapter 12
Terrorism Survival Precautions

A safe home involves more than just thwarting the common burglar, avoiding troublesome traffic problems, and steering clear of annoying nuisances. Today, a safe home is one that will safeguard you and your family from catastrophe, especially from the world's newest threat—terrorism.

Your home should have certain assets that will allow you to survive without being uprooted from your home because of an act of terrorism itself, or the widespread social disorder that could result from major or protracted events.

Social disorder, also known as civil or urban unrest, distinguishes itself from panic by not being immediate. Social disorder usually develops hours, days, or even weeks following an incident. It is often produced by a fear that our future is in jeopardy.

It is most pronounced by the hoarding of food and fuel, which creates a snowball effect. It is also marked by the breakdown of routines, which allows a variety of things to happen or not happen. Social disorder can also result in riots, looting, protests, and traffic jams.

Social disorder is a clear and present danger. In fact, when it comes to terrorism, the greatest threat lies in the possibility of social disorder triggered by fear. Therefore, it is essential that you recognize the potential for social disorder and that you prepare for its possible occurrence.

While a hurricane can be frightening, it is largely predictable. Forecasting determines its strength, strength potential, direction of travel, and when and where it is likely to make landfall. In contrast, an act of terrorism is highly unpredictable in every respect. In the event of a broad or serious act of terrorism or if multiple terrorism attacks occurred in succession, fear could spread quickly, creating an unstable situation that could easily lead to widespread and possibly prolonged social disorder.

Almost every American home is dependent to some degree on external utility sources for sustaining life. Some homes are very dependent. In the event of a major terrorist attack, utilities could become limited or nonexistent for anywhere from a few hours to a few months. Your ability to remain in your home is dependent on being self-sufficient. For example, in northern climates, winter cold can easily drive you from your home if you don't have a heat source that can operate without utilities or in the absence of fuel that is delivered to the home by truck or pipe.

It is important to give priority to those attributes that will allow you at least some degree of self-sufficiency in the event of utility disruptions. Consider the following:

If a prospective home has a fireplace or wood stove, consider it a big plus. Fireplaces and wood stoves are often sought after amenities for their aesthetic and sensory value; but should gas or petroleum supplies become short, a fireplace or wood stove will not only provide heat but will also allow you to boil (purify) water and cook meals. In cold climates, a fireplace or wood stove can mean the difference between living in your home and living in a shelter. At the very least, make sure your home has a wood stove hook-up so you can easily install a wood stove.

Homes on public water systems are best. However, if a prospective home has a drilled or even dug water well as a backup, it is important. Water is the single most essential ingredient to sustain life.

If public water supplies are contaminated or depleted or the infrastructure that delivers it by gravity or under pressure to your home is damaged or destroyed, your ability to continue to live there can be severely hampered.

Electrical power is important to almost every home in America. Its importance is not in its ability to power the coffee maker and hair dryer. Electricity's vital role is in heating and pumping water, firing furnaces, etc. If a home has a back-up electrical generator, it is a major asset, especially if it's permanently installed with a large fuel tank of 100 gallons or more. The best situation is when the generator is inconspicuously installed with noise suppression features and has an underground fuel tank. In the event of a major disaster, your power generation system and fuel supply will become targets of those who are without such benefits.

Homes with back-up alternative energy sources are also in a very good position. If a prospective home has solar power or power produced by a windmill, you will be better off than those who don't have an alternative energy source.

Communication is not always a necessity of life but can be very helpful and comforting during tough times. Because wired cable service could be interrupted like other utilities, a prospective home that has a satellite dish for receiving television transmissions is important. Likewise, a home with an old-fashioned rooftop television antenna for receiving broadcast television stations could become an important back-up system. Citizens Band (CB) and short-wave radio are free, effective, and little used communications systems. In addition, shortwave radio is a worldwide system. If a home has a scanner radio antenna, this is a security asset. Scanner radios allow you to keep abreast of what's happening elsewhere. Forearmed is forewarned.

Fuel Storage

In a full-blown terrorist attack, especially one that is long in duration, certain essential commodities, such as fuel, could become scarce. It is preferable that a home's fuel source be protected from theft. Oil tanks and propane cylinders that are located outside the home, especially if they are visible, are vulnerable.

If a home has dual fuel oil storage tanks or any arrangement than increases the amount of fuel oil that can be stored, consider it an asset. Having the ability to store 500 or more gallons of fuel oil might enable you to weather even a protracted fuel oil shortage.

Other Assets

Many American homes have cellars but a considerable number of houses are built on slabs or set off the ground on footings. In the event of a terrorist attack, a cellar can be a secure place not only for you and your family but also for the home's furnace, fuel oil storage tanks(s), water pump, and hot water heater. In very hot climates, cellars provide a cool place for the family and to some degree for perishables.

Bathtubs can provide effective shelter during a violent storm, like a tornado, and are very useful for storing a large quantity of pure water that could become vital.

Homes that have window coverings, such as working shutters or those that are stored and hung, can be of great value.

Homes with an open concept or design are not good during utility interruptions. Being able to close off all but one room is important if you are forced to use an alternative heat source. In addition, homes with traditional rooms offer better structural protection and security.

Chapter 13

Togetherness

One excellent way to prepare for the aftermath of terrorism is by getting together with your neighbors. This is a highly effective and efficient means of survival.

Neighborhood Watch groups or homeowner associations are perfect for establishing survival plans. If an existing group is too large, consider dividing into smaller groups of homeowners whose houses are in close proximity.

If no such groups presently exist in your neighborhood, consider forming a group for the purpose of developing a Neighborhood Survival Agreement.

The group could collaborate in a number of different ways. Consider working together to ensure the existence of all major amenities for your neighborhood as follows:

- At least one home should bear the responsibility of having a wood-burning fireplace or wood stove. A large stockpile of emergency firewood should be maintained.

- At least one home should purchase a portable generator and have a large emergency supply of fuel—at least 100 gallons.

- At least one home should have a fresh water well or stockpile bottled water.

- At least one home should have a television receiving satellite dish.

- At least one home should have a public safety scanner and a Citizens Band (CB) radio or short-wave radio with rooftop or tower antennas.

- At least one home should have a couple of cellular telephones with an adequate supply of fresh batteries.

- At least one home should have a high-speed Internet/e-mail connection.

- At least one home should have weaponry, such as a handgun or two and a rifle or shotgun. There should also be an adequate supply of ammunition.

- At least one home should have and maintain a supply of tran sistor radios and flashlights with an adequate supply of fresh batteries. There should also be a supply of matches, candles, and oil-burning lamps with an adequate supply of lamp oil.

- At least one home should stockpile a variety of canned and dry food and bottled water and be responsible for rotating it to keep it fresh.

- At least one home should stockpile medical supplies and specific groups of medicines.

One or more homes might already have these amenities.

Divide up whom will have what based on personal preferences, practicality, and the profession and/or experience of each member. For example, if someone in the group loves the aesthetics of a wood burning fire, he is the logical choice to have that amenity. A resident whose hobby is electronics might make a good choice as the "communications home." The stockpile of medical supplies and specific groups of medicine would ideally be the home of a physician. In contrast, a family with children would not be the home to have weaponry.

Put the Neighborhood Survival Agreement in writing, signed by all participants, and preferably notarized. It might be prudent to have it drafted or reviewed and executed by an attorney, particularly if there is a lawyer in your group.

In most emergencies, people have a tendency to pull together. However, in a major emergency it is possible that a "every person for himself" mentality will develop. In that case, the agreement will likely be useless. However, its very existence might be all that is required to ensure unity in your neighborhood.

In the absence of an existing group, such as *Neighborhood Watch*, start the process by determining what homes will constitute an obvious group. Groups should consist of at least five homes but preferably not more than ten. Proceed as follows:

• Start with an informal meeting at the home of a potential group member.

• Discuss the obvious amenities listed in Safe From Terrorism.

• Talk about other group specific and personal needs.

• Inventory what amenities already exist.

• Determine what each potential member is most comfortable contributing.

• Divide up who will do what.

Utilizing a neighborhood approach will also take care of the elderly, shut-ins, and those who are not financially or physically able to fully prepare their family and themselves.

Another reason for taking the neighborhood approach is to protect the stockpile of precious commodities.

It should be understood that at the very point when you're going to be dependent on those resources, you'd probably going to come under attack by those who want to part you from them, either for their own use or to sell on the black market. Consider the following:

- If water and food supplies were limited and you had plenty, what do you think would happen?

- If fuel supplies were depleted and you had a couple hundred gallons on hand, what do you think would be the result?

Therefore, when water, food, and fuel supplies are short and/or when looting is taking place, it may be necessary to have guards for protection, particularly at night. Having able-bodied guards on-duty up to 24 hours a day would be difficult or impossible unless it was a shared neighborhood effort.

Another benefit of the neighborhood approach is to maintain a sense of community, which can easily be lost when the emphasis is on security like it has been since 9/11. People have naturally become very leery of each other, which can in itself generate a feeling of uneasiness. A Neighborhood Survival Agreement could act as a catalyst for unity.

A group with a Neighborhood Survival Agreement with all the survival amenities in place will be in a very strong position to endure any crisis, even a long one.

It should be noted that apartment building occupants can form the same type of survival organization with some alternative features.

Chapter 14

Alternative Safe Havens

During and following an act of terrorism, it is imperative that you have a safe haven. While your home can often be that safe haven, there are times that it won't be feasible or safe. Therefore, you should have at least one alternative safe haven.

The ideal safe haven is one that is not near your primary home. It does little good to have a alternative safe haven that is a couple miles away because both could be vulnerable to the same act of terrorism.

An alternative safe haven should meet as many of the following criteria as possible:

• Located at least 100 miles from your primary home.

• Should not be more than 300 miles from your primary home.

• Should not have only one means of access.

• Must be accessible by motor vehicle.

• Should not be accessible by mass transportation.

• Must be located away from urban areas.

• Must be located away from predictable terrorist targets.

• Should preferably be located in an area that is geographically different from your primary home.

• Should be single-family occupancy.

• Should have the same survival amenities as your primary home.

Your alternative safe haven could be any or all of the following:

- **Family Home** – The home(s) of your parents, children, grand parents, grandchildren, and the like. Distant family relation ships could pose problems so they should be avoided.

- **Friend's Home** – Provided it is a close and dear friend. Lifelong friendships are best.

- **Second Home** – Always a preferred choice because you control it.

- **Vacation Home** – Like a second home, a vacation home is good.

If you don't have a safe haven that meets the stated criteria, there are alternatives that are better than having nothing. Consider the following:

- **Recreational Vehicle** – They can be situated just about any where and can be a home away from home wherever you park them. However, if they are parked at your home, their use will require you to return home to retrieve them, which may not be safe or possible.

- **Camping Site** – Having a designated camping site is okay provided it meets the criteria and the climatic conditions year round allow it to be used. Even if you don't keep your camping equipment with you, it is still possible that you could purchase what you need en-route to the camping site.

- **Designated Destination** – A designated destination, such as a motel or hotel, is better than nothing. However, vacancy is unpredictable and the lack of survival amenities may make such locations undesirable.

Once you have identified your alternatives safe haven(s), it is time to make solid arrangements with the primary occupants if applicable. This is not something to leave to chance. Even if it is the primary residence of close family, you need to have a solid understanding about the arrangement.

Remember, houseguests are an adventure for a day or two, but beyond that, they become a hassle. This is especially true if the alternative safe haven lacks enough bedrooms or if the core facilities, such as bathrooms, are limited.

It is best to have a reciprocal agreement with the owners of an alternative safe haven. Such an arrangement could cement the agree-ment. However, if your primary home is located in the city and your alternative safe haven is located in a rural area, it is doubtful that the dwellers of the alternative safe haven would ever need the shelter of your home.

The following apply to your alternative safe haven:

- Plan to go to your alternative safe haven sooner rather than later.

- Have at least two routes in addition to your preferred route to the alternative safe haven. Drive these routes occasionally so you are familiar with them. Make sure at least one route utilizes solely "back roads" or roads that are not numbered state highways.

- At least one of your routes should have a grocery and general merchandise store of at least moderate size on it. If you need equipment or supplies, this will allow you to purchase what you need without leaving a designated route and without wast ing time.

- Do not disclose the location of your alternative safe haven to other people.

Is your alternative safe haven in a rural area, especially a depressed one? Do you drive a late model Mercedes, Mercury Navigator, or similar vehicle? If so, it is a good idea to have an older, inconspicuous vehicle at your alternative safe haven. Why? Because vehicles like these tell people a lot about you. You don't necessarily want to be advertising your presence.
A gun should be at your alternative safe haven. Traveling with a gun is too dangerous, especially if you cross state lines.

Communications

Because every situation is vastly different, it is imperative to have a concrete understanding concerning when your alternative safe haven plan is triggered. Communications may be difficult or impossible during and after an incident, so preplanning is vital.

Ideally, you should establish two central communications "clearinghouse" houses. These houses should preferably be the residence of someone who is usually at home, for example, a retired individual or couple.

One "clearinghouse" house should be local and one should be far away where it is unlikely to be affected in anyway by the prevailing crisis. This is especially important when it comes to telephone service. If local telephone calling is affected, it is possible that long distance will work and visa-versa. Give all family members a wallet-sized list of the telephone numbers to carry with them at all times. Instruct them to call the local telephone number first. If they can't make contact, call the long distance number. Tape fifty cents (not a fifty cent piece) to the back of the cards to be used in the event that a pay telephone has to be utilized or that calling card services are down. It is also possible that landline telephones might be working and that cellular telephones might not be.

Plan Triggers

In the event conventional communications are not available, you must have designated plan triggers, which include the following (with the exception of direct contact, consider using multiple triggers to ensure that all family members are notified):

- **Direct Contact** – You may be able to talk directly with family members.

- **In-Direct Contact** – Messages left on answering machines or voice mail systems, e-mail you send, notes left at home or work, and messages left with neighbors.

- **"Clearinghouse" House Contact** – Messages relayed by the designated "clearinghouse" house contact person.

- **Declarations** – The newly established federal Homeland Security Advisory System is the most logical declaration to use. That system is as follows:

Low	Green	Low Risk of Terrorist Attacks
Guarded	Blue	General Risk of Terrorist Attacks
Elevated	Yellow	Significant Risk of Terrorist Attacks
High	Orange	High Risk of Terrorist Attacks
Severe	Red	Severe Risk of Terrorist Attacks

Your plan would most likely be triggered at the "High" level and certainly at the "Severe" level.

Other government issued declarations like a state of emergency issued by the Governor of your state, can be used to trigger the plan. Many states also have levels that relate to the seriousness of a situation. For example, minor, major, and catastrophic. These declarations will be widely reported. In addition, the federal government presently uses a range (1-4) of threat levels that determine the nature and scope of the Federal response.

- Evacuations – Voluntary or mandatory evacuations that are ordered in your area could be used to trigger your plan. These events are widely reported.

- Activations – Activation of your state's Emergency Operations Center (EOC) or the National Guard are widely reported events that indicate a serious situation. They could be used as plan triggers.

Chapter 15

Personal Arsenal

Wherever you go, you should always carry on your person the following items:

- Small flashlight with an extra battery.

- Small knife

- Whistle

- Pepper spray

- Cellular telephone

- Contact telephone number card with fifty cents (not a fifty cent piece) taped to the back.

- Two-way radios if you're with somebody and you might split up.

- Everybody who has a driver's license should have a set of keys or remote entry device to all the family vehicles.

Chapter 16

Home Arsenal

Assemble and keep intact a home arsenal. Duffle bags work best for storage because they can be easily carried without spillage. There should not be any need for long-term isolation, thus, the following items should be sufficient:

• Several battery operated flashlights with spare bulbs and extra batteries.

• A battery operated radio with extra batteries.

• A battery operated fan with extra batteries.

• A couple of cases of bottled water.

• A couple of large boxes of food bars.

• A bag of candy if you have children.

• A deck of playing cards.

• A first aid kit.

• A compact space blanket for each member of the family.

• Some large plastic trash bags and a roll of duct tape.

If you seek refuge with your home arsenal, try to take your cellular telephone if you have one. If applicable, take your child's handheld video games and stuffed animals, and any needed medications.

Chapter 17

Your Vehicle

Because we spend a lot of time in our vehicles and because they're indispensable forms of transportation, you should consider the following:

- Four-wheel drive vehicles are desirable.

- A second fuel tank is an asset.

- A second battery is beneficial.

- An on-board Geographical Positioning System (GPS) device is handy to have.

- Always treat a half full fuel tank as empty and re-fuel accord ingly. If you have a second fuel tank assume that you don't and re-fuel accordingly.

- Keep your vehicle in perfect condition. Have all required maintenance check-ups performed on schedule according to manufacturer recommendations. Check all fluid levels regular ly and keep them topped off. Make sure you have a full-size spare tire that's in good condition. Get a new battery every two years whether you need one or not. When repairs are needed, have it done immediately by a certified mechanic and specify that they use only new factory parts.

- Always keep a spare container of motor oil and windshield washer fluid in your vehicle along with an empty gas can and a set of jumper cables. Also make sure you have a first aid kit, a fire extinguisher, a simple tool kit, a blanket, a length of strong chain or rope, an ax, a shovel, and a box of sand.

Chapter 18

Health Precautions

If you haven't taken all possible health precautions, now is the time to start. Consider the following:

• Eat nutritious food and in moderation, take a multi-vitamin, drink at least eight 8-ounce glasses of water daily, exercise at least five times a week for at least thirty minutes, and wash your hands with soap and water regularly. If terrorism related hardship or sickness befalls you, you will have a much better chance of enduring it if you are healthy.

• Always get a flu shot, even if you are not in a high-risk group. The peace of mind alone is worth the effort and small expense of getting a flu shot. If you have flu like symptoms and you have had a flu shot, your health care provider will likely be quicker to order a test for other causes.

• If you are sick or injured in anyway and you think you should go or someone suggests you go to a doctor, then do so immediately.

According to the *Centers for Disease Control and Prevention (CDC)*, U. S. Department of Health and Human Services, it is not possible to get vaccines to protect against biological agents that might be used in terrorism. Vaccines for Anthrax are not recommended and are not available to the public. There is no vaccine against Plague; antibiotics will cure it. There is not enough small pox vaccine available. The CDC maintains a supply of antitoxin against botulism.

Chapter 19

Protective Precautions

The biggest threat at home from terrorism comes from foreign objects that you and others import. There are a number of protective precautions you can take regarding these items. Consider the following:

Mail

The United States Postal Service and the Occupational Safety & Health Administration – U. S. Department of Labor recommend that you always be observant for suspicious envelopes and packages and take the following mail precautions:

You should be suspicious of mail if one or more of the following factors exist:

• It is unexpected or from someone you don't know.

• It is addressed to someone no longer at your residence.

• It is handwritten, block printed, or poorly typewritten.

• The postmark does not match the return address.

• It has misspellings of common words.

• It has an incorrect title or has only a title.

• It has no return address or bears one that you can't confirm is legitimate.

• Its size or weight is unusual given its volume.

- It is lopsided, lumpy, or oddly shaped in appearance.

- It is sealed with excessive amounts of tape or string.

- It has protruding wires or aluminum foil.

- It is crystallized, discolored, or stained.

- It has a strange odor.

- It contains a powder or powder like residue.

- It is marked with restrictive endorsements such as "Personal" or "Confidential."

- It has excessive postage.

Consider taking the following precautions when processing mail:

- Don't handle a letter or package that you suspect is contaminated.

- Don't shake it, bump it, sniff it, blow into it, or empty its contents.

- Open mail with a letter opener that is least likely to disturb its contents.

- Open mail with a minimum amount of movement.

- Keep your hands away from your eyes, nose, and mouth while processing mail.

- Do an initial processing of your mail using gloves and a mask.

- Wash you hands thoroughly with soap and water when you are done processing mail.

- Do not lick stamps, stickers, and envelopes. Use self-adhering ones or a moistener device.

If you encounter a suspicious or contaminated piece of mail, do the following:

• Stay calm.

• Contact local law enforcement authorities.

• Don't shake it, bump it, sniff it, blow into it, or empty its contents.

• Keep your hands away from your eyes, nose, and mouth.

• Do not handle the envelope or package further or empty its contents.

• Isolate the letter or package.

• Do not move the envelope or package to another location.

• Do not move or remove any potentially contaminated items from the area.

• Seal off the room where the envelope or package is located until local law enforcement authorities arrive.

• Gently cover the letter or package with anything available nearby, like paper, clothing, or an inverted trash can, and do not remove the cover.

• If an unknown substance spills from the envelope or package, do not try to clean it up.

• Avoid creating air currents.

• Turn off air conditioners, fans, and portable heaters.

• Avoid tracking unknown substances.

• Wash hands with soap and water.

• Take a shower fully clothed. Remove clothes under water stream. Place all removed clothing in a trash bag or other container that can be sealed.

Remember, even a very thin envelope can contain a lethal or near lethal substance. Microelectronics has made possible letter bombs that are virtually as thin as an envelope containing a one-page letter.

Food

Inspect food, beverage, and water packaging carefully before purchase as follows:

- Make sure all factory seals are intact.

- Make sure it's not open or been opened.

- Make sure the packaging is not punctured, torn, or ripped.

- Make sure the packaging is not discolored or stained.

- Gently squeeze bagged products, like potato chips, to ensure a good seal.

- Tug lightly on cardboard flaps to make sure they're secure.

- Try the lids on all bottles and jars to ensure that they are tight.

Do not handle or buy items that appear to have been tampered with.

If you encounter food, beverage, or water that you believe is suspicious or contaminated, follow the precautions listed for when you encounter a suspicious or contaminated piece of mail.

Also take the following food precautions:

- Avoid brands or names you are not familiar with.

- Avoid imported items.

- Do not eat or purchase salad bar items.

- Do not partake of free samples.

- Wash thoroughly fish, fruits, vegetables, and all other applica ble food when you bring it into your home and before you pre pare or eat it.

- Unless you will be consuming food, beverage, or water within 72 hours, mark them with the date of purchase. In the case of food contamination, these dates could be important

Other Precautions

Consider taking the following precautions for other items that you bring into your home:

- Wash all clothing before you wear it.

- Wipe down all appliances and furniture before placing them

Chapter 20

Protecting Your Children

Being safe from terrorism is most important when it comes to our children. Our desire to keep them safe is second to nothing. So how do you ensure their safety? The best way is to keep them home; not in your house, but in the community where you live.

If you live in a safe community and your child largely remains in that community, he or she will be safer; and you will be blessed with a greater degree of peace of mind.

When To Say No

Regional, national, and even international trips for young people have in the past been quite numerous. It is rare that such trips are really necessary, especially after 9/11.

While these trips undoubtedly enrich the lives of participants, they do so with an unnecessary degree of risk.

You should carefully weigh each opportunity that arises for your child to leave home on field trips and other jaunts. More often than not, you need to say, "no," even if the school or other sponsoring organization is encouraging or requiring participation.

Destinations

Very often a distant location does not offer something that can't be found nearby, at least in some form. Ask yourself, have your children discovered their own backyards? Before letting your child travel a thousand miles to some distant location, ask yourself if they've partaken of all that your community, county, or state has to offer. Isn't there something that is just as good close by?

Chapter 21

When Your Children Leave Home

When it comes time for your children to leave the nest make sure you subject their destination to the same level of scrutiny that you have applied to your home. Beyond that, the best bet for ensuring they are safe from terrorism is to send them to private schools, summer camps, placements, and private residences that are in suburban or rural areas.

Be sure that their host organization is accredited. Accreditation itself does not relate directly to being safe from terrorism. However, accreditation means that an organization is above average. Which means that a multitude of safety related factors will be in your child's favor. If the accreditation process is voluntary, consider it an ace. That is because accreditation is a grueling process. Organizations that choose to be accredited and succeed in doing so are likely far above the rest.

Private Schools

Look for private schools that are accredited. There are several regional and national private school accrediting organizations in the country including the National Private Schools Association Group, Inc. (NPSAG) and the National Association of Private Schools (NAPS).

Summer Camps

If it is a summer camp (day, residential, or travel/trip) that you are contemplating sending Johnny to, you can ensure his safety to the maximum extent possible by simply choosing an American Camping Association (ACA) accredited camp. Less than one-third of the approximately 8,500 summer camps in the United States are accredited, but if the one you choose is, you have made a safe choice.

Placements

Hospitals, behavioral health care organizations, and group homes should have an accreditation from the Joint Commission on Accreditation of Healthcare Organizations (JCAHO) or the Council on Accreditation for Children and Family Services (COA).

JCAHO evaluates and accredits approximately 19,000 health care organizations and programs in the United States. According to JCAHO, accreditation "is recognized nationwide as a symbol of quality that indicates than an organization meets certain performance standards."

In 2001, COA accredited or was in the process of accrediting more than 1,400 public and private organizations that provide services to more than six million individuals and families in the United States and Canada. According to COA, their accreditation "is a process of evaluating an organization against best-practice standards."

Private Residences

Don't let your child visit, especially overnight, the home of family or friends unless you are convinced that the anti-terrorist measures in effect at your home exist there.

Organization Emergency Plans

Make sure you know and approve of the emergency plan for your child's school, summer camp, or placement. Emergency plans are diverse. Determine what the plan calls for in terms of when and how you will be contacted and when and where your child will be taken in the event evacuation is necessary. Are these consistent with your wishes and situation?

Make sure your emergency contact information is up-to-date. Be leery of plans that are dependent on telephone trees for contacting parents. This method can easily stop working if just one parent's telephone number is wrong or if just one parent fails to follow through by placing the next telephone call. If the emergency plan utilizes a central telephone number or the Internet for disseminating information, make sure you have the telephone number or World Wide Web site address with you at all times.

Also, make sure that the organization has your up-to-date employment telephone number, cellular telephone number, and other applicable telephone numbers including the one for your "clearinghouse" house.

Chapter 22

Shortages
The Principals of Supply and Demand

Shortages usually occur in advance of events, like a hurricane. While hoarding no doubt takes place, these types of shortages are generally good. They are simply people getting prepared. In fact, government officials sometimes advise people to prepare in this fashion before impending emergencies.

Shortages can be the result of hysteria, in which case they are self-induced. For example, even if there is no shortage, one can be quickly created if the mass media proclaims a shortage or the potential for one. It can also be fed by a "monkey see, monkey do" mentality.

A fresh example of supply and demand followed the 9/11 terrorism attacks. American flags became the symbol of choice to demonstrate sorrow, patriotism, and unity. Stores across the country quickly sold out of these items clearly illustrating the intensity at which shortages can develop. Shortages are most often limited to precious commodities, like food and fuel.

Shortages will become most acute in urban areas due to the greater population. To thwart personal shortages, consider doing the following:

- Maintain an adequate and fresh supply of basic emergency supplies.

- Seek extra emergency supplies immediately at the onset of any event that could trigger a shortage.

- If a shortage develops in your area, immediately contact family and friends at a distance and ask them to purchase in their locale whatever is in short supply in your area.

Chapter 23

Workplace Precautions

Workplace crime and violence and the potential for it are great. Each year between 1992 and 1996, more than 2 million U. S. citizens were victims of a violent crime while they were at work or on duty. These statistics will be increasing because terrorists are targeting workplaces, e.g., 9/11.

By taking a variety of measures, workplaces can be made safer. Make sure your employer follows these recommendations.

Environmental

- Unauthorized individuals should never be able to come and go freely. Personnel, electronic systems, or barriers should control all points of building ingress and egress that are not secure. If applicable, gates controlled by personnel or electronic systems should manage access to the grounds.

- Recorded surveillance systems should be employed and monitored

- Adequate lighting is essential in and around all buildings. Pedestrian plazas, walkways, parking lots, and all roads should be well lighted.

Administrative

- All employees, clients, vendors, and visitors should be required to wear appropriate identification badges at all times. The badges must be conspicuous at all times.

- There should be clear, open lines of communications within the entire organization. Encourage employee feedback and participation in all matters.

- There should be a strong, easily accessed, and free of cost employee assistance program.

- There should be stringent and strictly adhered to procedures for hiring, layoffs, downsizing, suspensions, and terminations.

- There should be early intervention policies and procedures for troubled employees who exhibit warning signs.

- There should be good severance packages for all employees with extended benefits.

- There should be good retirement benefits for all employees that never result in benefits being reduced.

- There should be a comprehensive crisis management plan.

Interpersonal

- There should be regular in-service training for employees at all levels aimed at helping them to recognize and respond to employees experiencing stress, those who communicate threatening remarks, and those who exhibit warning signs that could be a precursor to violence.

- Supervisors and managers should be adept at dealing with employees in a caring, sympathetic manner, regardless of the situation being addressed.

Chapter 24

Crisis Management Plans

There is no greater task incumbent upon an organization than the safety of those who walk through their doors. This includes employees, customers, vendors, faculty, students, and visitors. Therefore, the adoption of a comprehensive crisis management plan is essential. The chances of needing a crisis management plan is no longer remote; not having such a plan is simply unacceptable. During and immediately following an act of terrorism, a crisis management plan can mean the difference between manageable hardship and outright havoc. It can also be instrumental in aiding an organization's recovery from an act of terrorism.

Ask if the organization has a crisis management plan. If they don't, be leery, and ask why. If they do, ask to see it. Review it carefully for the following elements:

Purpose

The purpose of a crisis management plan is generally threefold.

- To protect the physical, mental, and emotional well being of all those present.

- To ensure that the pursuit of the organization's service goals takes place in an environment where those present feel safe.

- To safeguard the facility and its contents.

A comprehensive crisis management plan ensures that every crisis is responded to calmly, professionally, and promptly with as little inconvenience and disruption of business as possible.

In the case of terrorism, this level of response acts as a deterrent to future terrorism by eliminating or limiting the chaos and panic that deprives the terrorist of the gratification he is seeking. In addition, an event that receives this level of response won't leave those present wondering about the organization's ability to handle future, potentially more serious situations. In essence, a comprehensive crisis management plan not only makes people safer, it makes them feel safer.

Content

A crisis management plan should be written for the facility it represents. It shouldn't be a collection of generic information culled from different sources.

An organization's crisis management plan should be comprehensive enough to address every foreseeable event. Its contents will vary depending on a variety of factors specific to each organization; but generally, it should address every event that could result in the following:

• Jeopardize or eradicate the physical, mental, or emotional well being of those present.

• Result in substantial damage to the organization's facility or property or that could render the facility or the organization's property largely or wholly unusable.

Every crisis management plan should contain certain key elements, including, but not necessarily limited to, the following:

- An introduction and definitions.

- The composition, appointment, responsibilities, and training of the organization's crisis management team.

- Agreements, liaisons, and training with local public safety officials.

- Intelligence gathering, risk assessment, and methods of keeping staff informed.

- Types of accidental and security events and specific detailed responses for each.

- Staff training and participant drills.

- Evacuation plans, including designated on-site evacuation gathering places and off-site evacuation transportation and destination, and procedures for carrying out an efficient and prompt evacuation.

- Event aftermath planning and procedures including a comprehensive critique of the incident.

Chapter 25

Government Interference

Living in certain states can interfere with your ability to protect yourself. Find out what laws exist in your state that could limit or prevent you from doing what you feel is necessary to protect your family and yourself. The following are examples of government interference:

Gun Laws

Gun laws vary widely from state to state, county to county, and municipality to municipality. Do you think gun ownership and gun possession make you safer? Does it make you feel safer? Do you think that no gun laws or weak gun laws make places safer? If so, you need to analyze state gun laws.

According to Gun Control In The United States: A Comparative Survey of State Firearms Laws, an April 2000 project of the Open Society Institute's Center on Crime, Communities & Culture and the Funders' Collaborative for Gun Violence Prevention, Massachusetts and Hawaii have the strongest gun laws. On a scale of 100, they ranked 76 and 71 respectively. They are followed by California, Connecticut, Maryland, New Jersey, Illinois, and New York, all of which have moderate gun laws. If you live or visit any of these states, you ability to own and carry guns could be limited. In addition, in Washington D. C., it is illegal to own guns.

In contrast, if you live in or visit Maine, you will be in the state that ranked the lowest (-10). Not surprisingly, Maine is also home to one of several municipalities that have passed symbolic ordinances that require ownership of guns.

State Correlation

The top six places where terrorism occurs includes five states (New York, Florida, California, Maryland, and Illinois), and Washington D. C. Of these six places, five (excluding Florida) are ranked in the top nine places that have strong gun laws according to the report Gun Control In The United States: A Comparative Survey of State Firearms Laws.

Some schools of thought believe that gun legislation has been the catalyst of anti-government sentiment. This could make acts of terrorism more likely in states that have stringent gun control legislation.

Dog Laws

One of the greatest deterrents to attacks in any form is a dog. The same holds true for some forms of terrorism. In the aftermath of a terrorist incident, an effective watchdog could be vital if widespread social disorder were to develop.

Unfortunately, local and state governments are increasingly mandating stringent restrictions that make ownership of certain breeds costly and impractical.

Some local and state governments have also enacted or are considering enacting breed specific legislation to control what are believed to be dangerous dogs. Breed specific laws make the ownership of certain breeds or types of dogs illegal.

The breeds most often restricted or banned are as follows:

- Doberman

- Rottweiler

- Staffordshire bull terrier

- American pit bull terrier

- American Staffordshire terrier

- Any breed or mixed breed commonly known as a pit bull.

- Any breed or mixed breed having the appearance or character istics of a pit bull.

Not surprisingly, Dobermans and Rottweilers are among the best breeds for watchdog security and barking.

The American Kennel Club "strongly opposes any legislation that determines a dog to be 'dangerous' based on specific breeds or phenotypic classes of dogs."

While breed specific legislation has been deemed unconstitutional, these laws nonetheless exist. If you want to be safer and feel safer with the ownership of one of these attack-deterring dogs, find out if municipal, county, and state law allows you to own them without restrictions.

Freedom of Movement

The constitution permits that extraordinary measures can be taken for extraordinary threats. To prevent or respond to an act of terrorism, government officials have the authority to take actions that infringe on the constitution.

The governor of the affected state usually has sole authority to implement these measures. For example, the governor may be able to impose the following measures:

• Require that you evacuate your home.

• Require that you remain in your home.

• Prevent you from traveling by motor vehicle by closing public roads to civilian traffic.

• Limit or stop all public transportation.

• Close municipalities or counties, or sections thereof, to civilians.

• Limit or curtail utilities.

• Ration commodities.

Depending on the situations, these measures can also be employed during natural disasters like hurricanes or during widespread social disorder.

There are two important things to remember when the government declares a state of emergency, imposes martial law, or takes some other similar action than infringes on your freedom. First, urban areas, by their very nature, are usually the first and sometimes the only places where these restrictions will be imposed. The need to take these measures in other places, especially rural areas, is highly unlikely. In addition, when these restrictions are imposed in urban areas, officials who do not know you will likely vigorously enforce them. In fact, officials who have been assigned to the area from away may enforce them. Second, the government, especially in an urban area, may impose and enforce these measures with the premise that "the needs of the many outweigh the needs of one." This means that your individual freedoms and rights under such circumstances could be severely limited or nonexistent. The government enforcers will likely be blind to you or your situation, regardless of how dire it might be. These measures illustrate another reason why urban areas are not desirable for living, working, and visiting during times of terrorism.

Chapter 26

When Terrorism Occurs

There is no way for us to predict when a terrorist attack will occur. All we can do is analyze when they have taken place in the past.

A date/day analysis of 360 terrorist incidents, suspected terrorist incidents, and preventions in the United States from 1980-1999 revealed the following:

• 84, or 23 percent, occurred on the weekend.

• 276, or 77 percent, occurred on weekdays.

The following is a breakdown of the number of terrorist incidents, suspected terrorist incidents, and preventions that occur on each day of the week.

Day	Number
Sunday	41
Monday	71
Tuesday	56
Wednesday	38
Thursday	61
Friday	50
Saturday	43

In some cases multiple incidents occurred on the same date and in the same place. It should be noted that on Saturday, May 11, 1985, 13 attempted bombings or preventions took place in Baltimore, Maryland.

If this data were removed, the total for Saturday would be 30 terrorist incidents, suspected terrorist incidents, and preventions. This would mean that of the 347 terrorist incidents, suspected terrorist incidents, and preventions, Saturday accounted for only 8.6 percent.

This data are the primary bases for the suggestion that visiting an urban area is best done on weekends.

Chapter 27

Just Stay Home!

The world today is a dangerous place. Violence, and the potential for it, is everywhere. While proactive safety measures can make you safer and make you feel safer, the one sure-fire way to be your safest is to stay home. While the notion of staying home may sound somewhat bizarre, it's not.

First, lets qualify a couple of matters. Staying home doesn't mean that you never leave home. That's all but impossible. It does mean that to the extent possible, you become a homebody. Given the opportunities and technology that exist today, this is very possible.

Let's be hypothetical. If you were able to never leave your home, how safe would you be?

- Terrorism – Provided you presently live or decide to purchase a home in a fringe suburban area, which has historically been terrorism proof, you'll be as safe from terrorism as you possibly can be.

- Motor Vehicle Travel – Because you're home, you're not travel ing. Which means your chances of becoming one of the more than 40,000 people killed annually on the Nation's roads is less.

- Crime – You'll be safer from crime if you stay home, Consider the following:

- Rape/Sexual Assault – In 1999, 73.4 percent of all rape/sexual assault occurred in a place other than at or in the home.

- Robbery – In 1999, 84.4 percent of robberies occurred in a place other than the victim's home.

- Burglary – In 1999, significantly more residential burglaries occurred during daylight hours. This means if you're at home, there's a good chance your house won't be chosen.

- Theft – In 1999, 90.4 percent of all thefts occurred in a place other than at or in the home.

- Motor Vehicle Theft – In 1999, 98.8 percent of all motor vehicle theft occurred in a place other than at or in the home.

- Fire – If you're home, there's a greater chance you'll be able to prevent or detect early the 48.3 percent of fires that occur during the time a business day employee is out of the house.

Chapter 28

Alternating Your Lifestyle

Never leaving home isn't realistic for most people. It is also probably a recipe for insanity. Therefore, a more practical approach is to determine when, where, and how you leave your home.

At Home

Good methods for making purchases from the safety of your home include traditional catalog mail sales, shopping channels, and the Internet's World Wide Web.

On-line businesses that allow you to stay home include banking, bill paying, loan, brokerage, insurance, travel, and auction services, and a diverse array of entertainment sites such as games and gambling.

It is increasingly possible to work and conduct many forms of business from your home. Consider using the following methods:

- Telephone

- Fax

- E-mail

- Internet

- Intranet

- Courier

• Private delivery services

Avoid Urbanity

Just as you shouldn't live in an urban area, you should avoid visiting them if you can. While this may sound ridiculous and impossible, consider doing the following:

Avoid doing business with enterprises that only have inner city offices. Most companies have branch or satellite offices in suburban areas. Instead of traveling into the city, travel to a suburb. With the array of technology available, it should not be difficult for the company to offer all their services at a branch or satellite office.

Many professionals, such as psychiatrists, physicians, dentists, attorneys, and accountants have tired of city life and have moved to the suburbs where they now practice. When searching for a professional, make a suburban location one of the selection criteria.

Conducting Business

As indicated, information technology, such as telephones, faxes, e-mail, the Internet, and intranets can replace the need to travel in almost all circumstances. Couriers and overnight delivery services can handle the rest.

Videoconferencing equipment is quickly becoming a viable alternative to travel.

When you must get together, consider alternate ways. For example, instead of you traveling to the company headquarters in an urban area, meet your contact halfway in a small urban or suburban area.That way the distance you travel will be less and you will stay out of urbanity.

Selective Visits

If you must venture into an urban area, consider doing the following.

- Request an appointment during non-business hours—before 9:00 a.m. or after 5:00 p.m. The earlier before 9:00 a.m. and the later after 5:00 p.m. the better.

- Request Saturday appointments. These are often available.

- Request a rendezvous at a location of mutual convenience. For instance, ask the other person to meet you halfway at a library, hotel, restaurant, or other location that is mutually convenient.

- If it's a leisure visit, plan to go during the weekend.

- Avoid visiting urban areas on major holidays.

- Avoid urban areas at any time when special events are taking place. These include the following:

- Visits by politicians, government leaders, dignitaries, and celebrities

- Major athletic events

- Big concerts

- Important fundraisers

- Parades

- Large funerals

When You Go Out

From the time you leave your home until the time that you return you need to have the right mind set. You need to develop habits. To simplify things, the matters you need to pay attention to and the actions you need to take follow in chronological order.

Before You Leave Home

• Is your alternative safe haven plan up-to-date?

• Do you have your personal arsenal items?

• Does the vehicle you're using have at least half a tank of fuel?

• If highway travel conditions are available, have you checked them? Many transportation authorities now offer up-to-date telephone, radio, television, Internet, and sign board advi sories.

• Will you pass or remain in close proximity to any known terror ist targets?

As You Are Traveling

• Have you encountered any highway advisories or sites that could delay or block your path home or to your alternative safe haven?

• Have you noticed any potential terrorist targets on your route?

• It may sound redundant, but avoid road rage and the behaviors leading to it like the plague. You just never know whom you might cross paths with.

• When traffic is heavy, drive in right lanes to avoid being boxed in.

• In bumper-to-bumper traffic, don't ride the bumper of the vehi cle ahead of you. Leave room to turnout should the need arise.

Parking Your Vehicle

• When you park your vehicle, back it into a well-lighted parking space on the fringes of the parking lot to allow for an easy exit.

- Do not use parking garages or parking areas that are under ground. If no ground level, open-air parking lots exist, arrive at your destination with sufficient time to find on-street parking, even if it means walking several blocks or more.

- Park you vehicle where you can exit easily. For instance, the last parking space before an intersection controlled with a traf fic signal. This will likely prevent you from being boxed in and you won't be dependent on others to proceed because the traf fic signal will provide you with control.

In Establishments

- Ask for or select a seat that is near an exit or an emergency exit. If possible, sit near an exit or emergency exit that is near where you have parked your vehicle.

- Identify all other emergency exits and the location of other exits like delivery, maintenance, kitchen, and stage doors, and loading docks.

- Ask for or select a seat that allows your back to be against the wall so you can observe all that is taking place in the establish ment.

- If you're above or below ground level, make note of where the stairways are located. There should be at least two stairwells.

- Don't use elevators. All buildings are required to have stair ways. Use them. If the building has too many floors, arrange an alternative place or use a service that will go to the building for you.

- Avoid crowded areas.

- Be constantly observant while in an establishment.

Chapter 29

Curtailing Travel

Following an episode of terrorism, many people change their travel plans. They opt to stay home or close to home. That's understandable. What isn't understandable is why people forget so quickly. If the actions you take following an event like an act of terrorism make sense for a week or a month, why do they stop making sense after that? The threat level definitely does not diminish with time. It very well could increase.

When you're traveling, your family and you are at greater risk. Here's why:

- You become far more dependent on people.

- You probably do not know what is in your path or at your desti nations.

- You cannot subject your path and destinations to the level of scrutiny necessary.

- You are cutoff to varying degrees from your family, friends, and support network.

- Your family will be without you.

- You are away from your home's survival amenities.

- You are likely further from your alternative safe haven home.

- You could become stranded, unable to return home.

Therefore, you should consider permanently curtailing all unnecessary travel, both for you and your family. If you must travel, consider the following:

The next two sections will examine control and self-evacuation and finality in greater depth. Speed speaks for itself.

Control

The nay Sayers would maintain that on 9/11 about as many people died in motor vehicle accidents on the Nation's roads as there were on the aircraft that were commandeered. While that is true, the issue here is the degree of control to protect oneself. When you are aboard a commercial airliner, there is precious little that is within your control. Consider the following, all of which are not within your control:

• The age, condition, and maintenance of the aircraft.

• The condition and competence of the airline's mechanics.

• The condition and expertise of the pilots.

• The condition and ability of the flight crew.

• The age, condition, and maintenance of the air traffic control system.

• The condition and skill of the air traffic controllers.

• The list of passengers on board.

• The degree of passenger security screening.

• The types of cargo allowed on board and the security screening of it.

• The security equipment and measures on-board the aircraft.

• The direction, elevation, and speed of the aircraft and other matters relating to the operation of the aircraft.

• The decision to delay departure, change course, or land prior to reaching the intended destination.

- The impracticality of knowing the weather conditions that will be encountered during the entire flight and the ignorance pos sessed by most air travelers regarding what weather conditions pose enough of a threat to cancel or delay the flight.

Now contrast this list of uncontrollable air travel factors with the list of controllable motor vehicle factors. When you are done with the comparison, the difference should be clear. When you travel by motor vehicle, you are most in control. When you travel by air, you have virtually no control.

- The age of your vehicle.

- Whether your vehicle has a valid state safety inspection sticker.

- Whether you allow your pre-teen to ride in the front passenger seat that is airbag equipped.

- Whether you fail to place a baby or toddler in an approved child restraint seat.

- Whether you don't install the child restraint seat properly.

- Whether you fail to place a child under age eight in an approved booster seat.

- Whether you install the booster seat properly.

- Whether you're excessively tired.

- Whether you're under the influence of alcohol or drugs.

- Whether you're operating over the posted speed limit, failing to stop fully for stop signs, and/or committing other seemingly minor traffic offenses.

- Whether you're allowing yourself to be distracted by others.

- Whether you're adjusting the radio or the tape or CD player.

- Whether you're responding to pager activation or using a cellu-lar telephone.

- Whether you're fiddling with or fishing for something.

- Whether you've ventured out during inclement weather.

Self-Evacuation and Finality

Self-evacuation and finality are vital travel factors.

When your mode of travel is on the ground, you have the best chance of survival. In other words, when you're on the ground, you have a chance to free yourself and walk away. You might be thrown free. Civilians in the immediate vicinity or public safety workers who may arrive within minutes might rescue you.

When you're in the air, underground, or on the water, you stand the greatest chance of dying a terrorist attack. Principally, this is because should you survive the initial event, you still have to contend with the dangers inherent to being in the air, underground, or on the water.

At 30,000 feet in the air your only chance of survival is to remain, perhaps for a long time, in the midst of danger. Likewise, 100 feet below street level in a dark tunnel, or a mile from shore in choppy seas, your chances of freeing yourself or being freed are at their worst. If you happen to achieve separation, your destined to die at worse, or at best you will still be in a perilous situation.

Chapter 31

When Terrorism Strikes

The chances of being directly affected by an act of terrorism are small. The greater threat comes from two sources: the panic that could ensue immediately following a terrorist attack and the social disorder that could unfold in the hours, days, and weeks that follow.

If You Are There

If you find yourself in the midst of a terrorist attack, there will be a multitude of circumstances that will dictate what you do and when to do them. Plan to follow prescribed emergency procedures—those that you have been trained to do, those that are posted, and those that are broadcasted or communicated to you by officials. Beyond that, the following general rules apply:

- Stay calm. You can't think if you are in a panic. If you panic, you become part of the mass panic. You become part of the problem. Hysteria is contagious; you will also be adding to the problem.

- Don't enter elevators under any circumstances. Always use stairwells.

- If crowd back-ups occur in stairwells or at exit points or if you see or sense danger ahead, use other exits if they are safe.

- Don't leave designated evacuation routes unless the problem ahead is significant and you are convinced based on doing so is prudent. Consider using delivery, kitchen, and maintenance doors, and loading docks.

- When you are clear of an evacuated building, quickly move away. Far away. Don't stop for any reason until you are at least several blocks away, preferably further. Here is why:

- You might block the free flow of others leaving the area.

- You could hamper the efforts of public safety workers who are arriving in the area and entering the building.

- Utility lines—gas, electric, sewer, and water—could or might become severed creating dangerous situations.

- Falling debris, such as glass and masonry, are a major hazard, especially in an explosion.

- Things may initially seem safe when you exit a building. However, wind, and vibrations from trains, subways, aircraft, and secondary explosions or shocks can dislodge debris or cause new damage.

- It is especially important not to believe that when you reach public safety workers—police and fire—that you are safe. You are not. They have other missions. In addition, terrorists may have a second attack planned that is designed to occur after the arrival of public safety workers with the sole purpose of targeting them.

- As an absolute last resort when you cannot evacuate the building or position yourself for evacuation, consider going to the basement. Find a small area away from utilities and dangerous materials; make sure the area has supporting walls nearby. Try to get under a solid object like a desk.

Panic

Panic is a real and frightening possibility in any act of terrorism. This is especially true when people are already anxious. Panic is usually the result of people who believe they are in imminent danger and want to remove themselves from that peril. The least threat of panic is when you are at home.

The greatest threat exists when you are in an urban area and in the midst of many people.

Example

You are at a sports stadium, where the attendance is greater than 50,000. You hear and see a small explosion at ground level at a point far away from you. Other than a whiff of smoke, you are not affected directly by the explosion. However, if the explosion is viewed as a terrorist act or if the crowd feels that another explosion may occur, panic could easily develop.

The greatest advantage in a panic situation is threefold. Do the following:

• Have a contingency plan, you are ill prepared without one.

• Stay calm, because few people will.

• Don't be a follower, others will, and proceed cautiously.

Have A Contingency Plan

Wherever you go and whatever you are doing, always have a contingency plan. Contingency plans should include the following:

• Two places where you will meet should you become separated.

One place, called the local place, should be in or around where you are. For example, at an amusement park, the main gate or your vehicle.

The second place, called the distant place, should be far removed from where you are. The distant place could be some where on the outskirts of an urban area or it could be home. The important thing is that it be at a great enough distance so that it will likely not be affected by the terror crisis.

Be explicit about where you will meet under various circum stances. Discuss the possibilities. Because of a variety of vari ables, this cannot be set in concrete. However, the situation itself and common sense will most often make the rendezvous location obvious.

It is important to remember that if you become separated, you should proceed calmly to the appropriate meeting place. Do not waste time searching for others, pets, and belongings. Never return to where the trouble is or could be. Determine the appropriate, fastest route of travel to the meeting place and walk there. Once you are there and safe, stay there.

It is vital to have regular family discussions about these matters, especially with children.

Stay Calm

It is natural to become excited when an unusual event takes place, especially when we feel our safety or the safety of our family is at risk. However, the worse thing you can do is to get upset. You must stay calm at all cost.

To help you stay calm during a crisis do some advance work. Think about the times you have read or watched a troubling situation unfold. Have you wondered why the characters involved couldn't see what was coming or why they didn't do the obvious thing or make a better choice? It is because they were too caught up what was happening. To stay calm, you need to be apart from the prevailing madness, not a part of it. Visual yourself in various crisis situations. How would you feel? How would you act? What would you do? What would be best?

Don't Be A Follower and Proceed Cautiously

To avoid becoming a part of the panic, you need to resist becoming a follower. If possible and prudent, take actions that are the direct opposite of what the crowd is doing. Also, you should proceed with caution. Consider the following:

- In a facility, the crowd will often try to exit the same way they entered.

- If it seems practicable, leave your location in the opposite direction of the crowd.

- If practicable, consider exiting through kitchens, stages, shipping areas, receiving points, and loading docks.

- Always walk, do not run.

- Being first is not always an advantage. In most cases, yielding to others is prudent.

- Don't allow yourself to become immersed in a surging crowd even if it means dropping back and losing ground. Remember, being crushed is a real possibility than can kill.

- In a panic, handholding is not just for children. All family members should hold hands.

- If you can't hold hands, walk single file in close contact.

- If feasible and necessary, place your hands on the shoulders of those in front of you.

- Place children between adults.

- Carry small children and pets.

- Read the path ahead as you proceed.

- Are there any dangers present? Is the crowd building up? If so, can you change direction?

- If you are above ground, do not go underground.

- If you are underground, try to come above ground.

- Stay away from structures higher than you are; they could crumble or topple.

- Try to stay surrounded by structures somewhat lower than you that provide concealment.

- Look all around you constantly. Look up for visible utilities— wires, transformers—and for debris that may be falling.

- Look down at the surface ahead for damage, especially utility damage.

- Your destination should always be a safe, crowd free, open-air location.

- If it is not practicable, don't make your destination your car or the boarding point of the mass transportation you used.

- If you are separated when the incident occurs or if you become separated following the incident, revert to your contingency plan.

Chapter 32

Analyzing Acts of Terrorism

When terrorism strikes, you need to consider a variety of factors that will allow you to continue to safeguard your family and yourself. First, get answers to the following questions as quickly as possible:

Questions That Need Answering

Who is to blame or who could be blamed?

- What organization was responsible?

- What organization claimed responsibility?

- What organization is suspected of being responsible?

- What organization could have assumed responsibility?

What is the make-up of the organization?

- What is the nationality of the organization?

- What is the nationality of the perpetrators?

What was the intent of the organization?

- What organization did they oppose?

- What was their purpose?

- What cause did they oppose?

- What were they trying to stop?

- What was their message?

When and where did it occur?

- When did it occur?

- Where did it occur?

Once you know the answers to these questions, you should immediately analyze the information to determine your level of risk. Start with your neighborhood.

Neighborhood

Does anyone who could be targeted live in your neighborhood? For example, do you have neighbors whose nationality matches those responsible for the act of terrorism? Do you have neighbors who may not be of the same nationality but could be confused with people who are terrorists because of language, dialect, mannerisms, skin color, dress, furnishings, ornaments, or activities?

Do you have a neighbor who supports or works for an organization that is directly or indirectly connected to the act of terrorism?

Community

Are there any establishments in your community that could be targeted because of their ethnic profiles? Are there any establishments in your community that represent or serve the same purpose as the one targeted in the act of terrorism?

For example, if an abortion clinic was the target, are they any abortion clinics in your community? If the target was a Jewish establishment, are there any Jewish establishments in your community?

Widen The Scope

Continue with this analytical process by widening the scope of analysis to include where you work, where your children go to school, where you shop and use services, and where you go on business and for entertainment and vacations.

Remember to include all family members. If you have a daughter at private school or a son who is away at college, bring them into the loop of this process; they need to subject their settings to the same analysis.

It is of particular importance to stay away from areas that have ethnic affiliations or identities. For example, many cities have sections that are dominated by certain nationalities and their cultures. These areas are usually well known. People seeking revenge will likely be attracted to these areas.

When Your Family Or You Fits The Bill

There is a possibility that a member of your family or you will fit the bill or have a characteristic that could make them or you the target of revenge for terrorism. Your immediate reaction might be that taking precautions is unnecessary or that you are not going to let your life be interrupted by external events. These are foolhardy positions to take. Depending on the situation, the threat could be real. This is not a time to be proud.

Consider doing the following at least until you can make a determination concerning the level of risk that exists:

- Be vigilant. If you hear or see anything or anybody suspicious, report it to the police immediately.

- If you receive a threat, no matter how veiled, report it to the police immediately.

- If you are in a hostile area, consider retreating to a friendlier area.

- Limit the out of home activities of your children.

- When you leave home, do the following:

  - Forego wearing clothing or jewelry that could be interpreted as having a connection.

  - Don't speak your native language.

  - Stay in your area.

  - Stay together.

  - Patronize only establishments where you are known.

- Consider joining the prevailing national symbolism. For instance, following the terrorist attacks of 9/11, displaying any flags became popular. However, proceed with this cautiously. Depending on the situation, this could cause a hate crime against.

- Decline media interviews, which will put you in the spotlight.

Appendix

Research Staff
Hanrow Press

The events of 9/11 were pre-designed to effect massive numbers of American citizens. The usual format of foreign terrorism is designed to kill small numbers of persons usually from one to several dozen persons. It is predictable that the terrorists will eventually choose single individuals, families or people in casual settings such as shopping malls, schools, etc. The plan is to create fear at the everyday level of American life.

The prudent American is going to have to adjust his thinking to small and local approaches rather than anticipating massive terrorist attacks.

We know that Saddam Hussein some years ago purchased 12 portable aerosol generators. These could be placed on the back of a small truck. Various chemical and biological compounds could easily be sprayed from such trucks. Obviously you do not want to be the fellow following such a truck with your vehicle.

The terrorist nuclear threat is generally imagined as a big nuclear device capable of a vast nuclear explosion. Such a weapon is rather sophisticated and requires a good delivery system such as a relatively large airplane or a missile. What is more likely is what is called a "dirty nuclear bomb." This is where a conventional explosive, such as dynamite, is exploded but has non-bomb radioactive material associated with it. Fine radioactive materials would spread like confetti in the air.

It has to be assumed that homegrown American psychopaths will copy some of the foreign terrorist behaviors. Fortunately you don't have to be initially concerned as to the nationality of a terrorist.

You are now beginning to see the greatest terrorist threats other than human fear. In Part II of the book we will explore some more important things you must do to protect yourself, your family and your friends.

Bioterrorism

It is very difficult to spread a biological substance such as anthrax in open areas. Thus, it is wise to stay away from confined areas such as subways, tunnels, elevators, etc.

As when miners took canaries into mines to provide early detection of toxic gases, we Americans have our own "sentinels" for detecting bioterrorism substances. 110 million cats and dogs live with us in America. Your dog or cat will show signs of the illness before you do. If you don't have such a pet, we strongly suggest you get a dog or car. They are also great stress relievers.

Some strains of laboratory mice are early detectors of anthrax as are guinea pigs and New Zealand white rabbits. Such animals are called "disease sentinels: they will usually show signs of anthrax infection several days before a human will. It takes fewer anthrax spores to infect these animals.

The current anthrax detection equipment is very expensive, hundreds of thousands of dollars. Home kits may become available.

C

Do not believe our water supplies are well guarded, they are not! Fortunately the chlorine and other chemicals utilized in water purification plants will kill most biologicals or other substances in the water. Water purification does through a good number of steps. The final filtration step is where the terrorist substance would have to be added. Usually on plant personnel have access to the final stage of purification. Do not take anything for granted. **Convert to buying or having delivered only steam processed distilled water.** Most so-called "spring" waters do not actually come from springs; much is just rebottled and filtered tap water. Water purified by osmosis will not do.

Gas mask type protection has become a heated topic of debate. Unfortunately there are loads of old and also fake gas masks available. We strongly that your only purchase gas masks that are made in Israel where they have been designed to protect against a host of airborne assaults. We do know that our enemies are producing cyanide gas at phosgene and chlorine gases.

An alternative mask is high-efficiency particle filtration mask (HEPA).This will be expensive.

Warning: if you have a beard or a bush mustache, a gas mask may be of little use. To be effective, a gas mask must have a tight fit on the face. Mustaches and beard commonly prevent such a right fit.

An important consideration concerns children, especially the very young. Little to nothing is known about how biotechnical weapons can affect children. Be-

D

ing small, young children will likely be more effected by such agents. They will likely also be more vulnerable to any agents that have settled to the ground since they are physically closer.

Equipment You Need

You need to have a good supply of the following:

- **Latex powder free examination gloves –** Be sure you are not allergic to latex. You can obtain these at drugstores and discount clubs.

- **An extensive first aid kit**

- **A power generator**

- **Minimally one month supply of steam distilled drinking water**

- **3 month supply of all prescription medications** and over-the-counter medications

- **Four months supply of canned and frozen foods**

F

You may also want to investigate the installation of a home and/or office air filtration system that eliminates all biological agents.

G

Food Away From Home

We know of several homegrown acts of terrorism involving food supplies. Some of these acts has been committed in restaurants, some in grocery stores and some at salad and food bars.

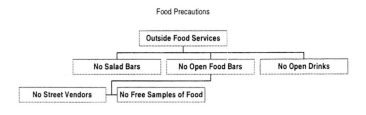

H

Food at Home

The following rules must be strictly followed:

- **Do not purchase any fruits that have tears or other openings on or in their outer skins**

- **Remove the outer 1/3 of all leafy vegetables – soak and wash thoroughly**

- **Wear latex gloves while washing food and then dispose of the gloves**

Warning: Eco-saboteurs such as animal rights activists and earth-liberation types will be stepping up attacks on farms, fast food restaurants, laboratories, and governmental facilities. We may have to deal with homegrown and foreign terrorists.

I

Security at Home

Doors and Locks

Solid core doors provide significantly greater protection for houses and apartments. Hollow core doors are very easily kicked and knocked in. The greatest protection is afforded by the solid steel door, next by the reinforced hollow core steel door. All solid core wooden doors should minimally be 1¾ inches thick. A flush door is much better in terms of protection than a panel door. Very often panel doors are used because they are decorative. The security problem related to the panel door is that the panels often are not very thick, at least not as thick as the flush part of the door; these panels can be easily kicked and knocked in. **Solid core panels should minimally be ½ inch thick.**

J

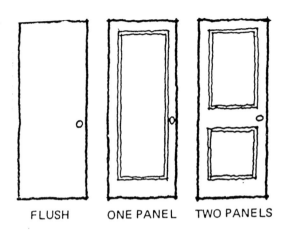

FLUSH   ONE PANEL   TWO PANELS

Door Types

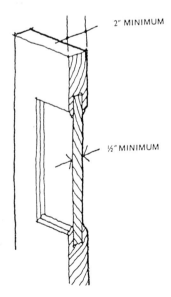

2" MINIMUM

½" MINIMUM

Panel Door

K

A door often will not provide greater protection than the doorframe, which holds it in position. Generally wooden frames are a poor choice of materials. **If wooden frames are used, they should be minimally 2 inches in thickness. Metal frames provide a very high level of protection,** followed by metal clad wood doors. A hollow core steel door should be filled with cement.

The door, which swings outward, should have a protective angle iron, which will aid in the prevention or tempering with the door strike. Other doors should have rabbeted jambs, which will protect the door strike. The door that swings outward should have an escutcheon plate.

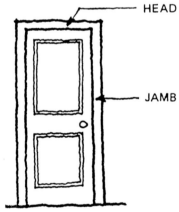

Door Frame

L

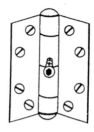

Nonremovable Hinge Pin

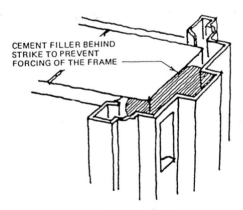

CEMENT FILLER BEHIND
STRIKE TO PREVENT
FORCING OF THE FRAME

Hollow Metal Door Frame

M

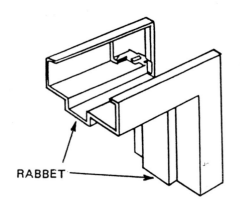

RABBET

Rabbeted Jamb

There are also available various types of bullet-proof steel doors.

Hydraulic jacks, such as car jacks, can be used to spread the doorframe springing the entire door. Even a heavy steel door if mounted in a wall, which is drywall, is not good protection from a terrorist who may resort to kicking in the drywall. Masonry or reinforced wooden walls will likely deter the terrorist.

All doors in an office or apartment building should have spring or electric closers to prevent the terrorist from following tenants or visitors into the building. **Hinges must be placed on the inside** to prevent the terrorist from removing hinge pins and eventually the doors. Non-removable hinge pins should be used.

The mortise lock is housed which is housed in the door itself. The lock must contain a deadbolt which is key-operated from the outside. You can also purchase a mortise lock which is also key operated from the inside; this type may be counterproductive if you have to make a quick exit and not be able to find the key to open the deadbolt from the inside. The door should not have any windows.

O

The deadlatch type of stopwork has an automatic system which keeps the latch projected against the strike plate. This type of system is very prone to attack through the use of credit cards and hangers. The deadlatch must be used in conjunction with a deadbolt.

The key-in-knob type of lock is to be avoided.

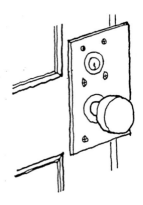

Escutcheon Plate for Doors Opening Out

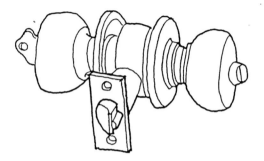

Key-in-Knob Lock

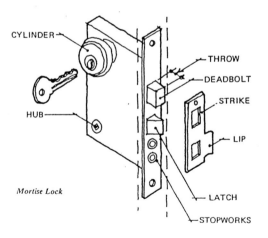

Mortise Lock

CYLINDER

THROW

DEADBOLT

STRIKE

HUB

LIP

LATCH

STOPWORKS

Q

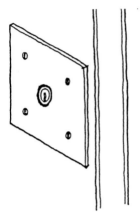

Escutcheon Plate Covering Cylinder Mortise Lock

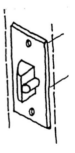

Deadlatch

R

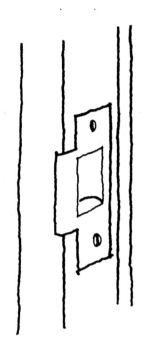

Door Strike

    Spring bolt, vertical bolt and horizontal bolt locks are to be used as supplementary or secondary locks. These devices provide additional security. The vertical bolt deadbolt is preferred since it involves two deadbolts and can also have a pickproof cylinder. Never should any of the supplementary locks be used a primary locks.

Maximum security can be achieved through the use of the buttress door lock. It has a steel bar, which is held in a floor receptacle and the double bar lock, which extends into the doorjamb.

One of the best locks is the Abloy type; it has a round key which is specially cut and usually can only be duplicated by use of a registration number. There are also magnetic cylinders. **Cylinders should have minimally 5 pins** and should be protected from the outside by spinner rings or an escutcheon plate.

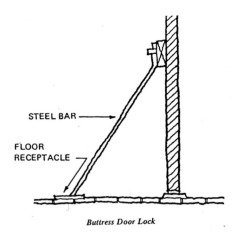

STEEL BAR

FLOOR
RECEPTACLE

Buttress Door Lock

T

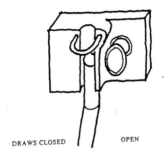

DRAWS CLOSED   OPEN

"Magic Eye" Lock with Thumb Turn

Spring Bolt

U

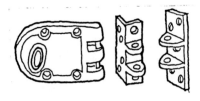

Vertical Bolt

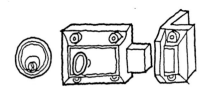

Horizontal Bolt

V

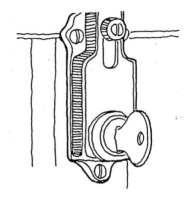

Loxem Sli-door Lock

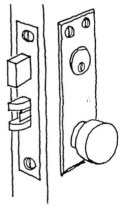

Antifriction Latch Bolt

W

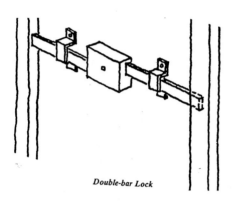

Double-bar Lock

Protective Angle-Iron for Doors

X

Protective Angle-Iron for Doors

Y

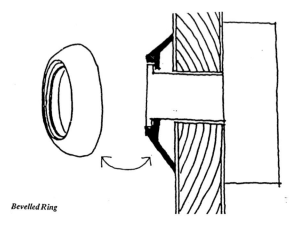

Bevelled Ring

Spinner Ring

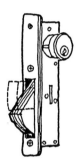

Segal Lock

In the case of patio sliding doors, the movable portion should be on the inside; the door should have break proof glass. There should be a vertical Segal lock or a Loxem lock. Any sliding glass or exterior glass door should be able to resist 300 pounds of horizontal force.

Double doors should have flush bolts and a mortice bolt system that requires a key.

Building exit doors should be self-closing and should open only out to the exterior. All exit doors should have anti-friction latch bolts.

AA

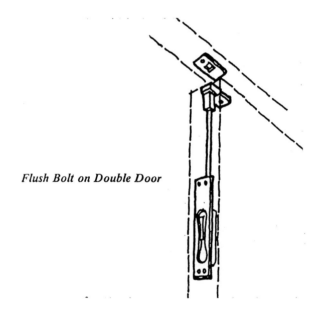

Flush Bolt on Double Door

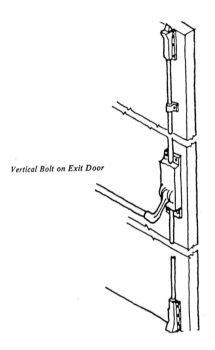

Vertical Bolt on Exit Door

Peepholes

      Apartment and home front doors shoulᵤ ᵢve peepholes. The problem is that a regular peephole provides an excellent channel for a bullet. The peephole should have an inexpensive closed circuit video system. These are readily available from security supply companies. These devices enable you to see who is outside the door without risking death. The closed circuit TV peephole is usually very easy to install. Peepholes should be located 4 ¾ inches above the floor. If using a regular peephole, make sure the peephole is a wide angle one.

Door Chain Locks

These devices are useless

Garage Doors

Steel garage doors provide the greatest protection. Electric garage door systems offer great security. Slide bolts should be used at the bottoms of manually operated garage doors.

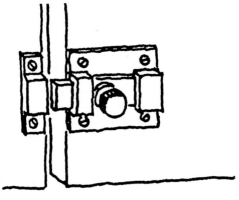

Slide Bolt on Garage Door

DD

Elevators

Elevators should not have emergency stop buttons; if they are present, they should be disabled. Elevators should have closed circuit TV. Elevators should also have convex mirrors so you can see if someone is hiding in the elevator.

Window Locks

Ground level and basement windows are very prone to attack. Top floor and stairwell-fire escape windows are the next easiest to invade. If break proof glass is not installed, locks are the next best item. The most common window lock is the crescent sash lock. Thumbscrew and pin latch locks are also to be used. **The only secure window lock is a keyed window lock.**

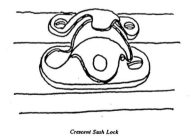

Crescent Sash Lock

Keyed Window Lock

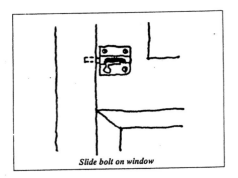

Slide bolt on window

Pin Latch

FF

Alarms

There are several types of alarms: contact devices, lock alarms, heat-sensitive, ultrasonic, photoelectric and laser beam. The most common types of alarms have a contact switch on a door or window. When the door or window is opened, the electrical circuit is interrupted and an alarm circuit is activated.

Another very common variation is the metal (foil) strip alarm. Foil strips are prone to damage and physical breakdown. Motion detection devices are also common. The sounds and lights of an activated alarm system may not deter a terrorist. If you have had a good number of false alarms, central security personnel may not take the alarm signal as being an emergency. Remember, the terrorist does not care whether he is detected as long as he achieves his goals.

A National Rifle Association decal on each of your doors may be a better deterrent.

You should also have available in your home an alarm activation device that you can activate before entry takes place.

GG

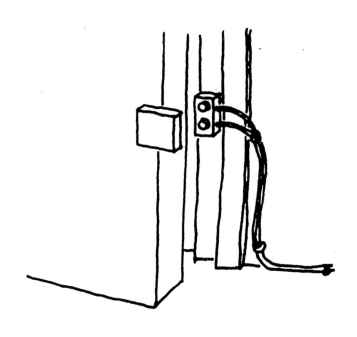

Contact Switch on Door

HH

Security Zones

Wherever you live, you must look at your security from terrorism as a series of security zones and layers of these zones. Whether you own a house or live in an apartment building, you or a security professional **must conduct a security survey.**

Every building and parking lot has particular zones of access. Level 1 is where the general public can enter the building. Level 2 is where the general public is excluded from entry. Level 3 is where only employees or residents of the building are allowed to enter. Level 4 is where only high-level employees or residents are allowed to enter the building or complex.

Zone and access control can be accomplished by the following:

- Security guards checking identification
- Special keys to special locks
- Push button/code entry systems
- Magnetic card entry systems
- Thumb print identification systems
- Iris (of the eye) identification systems

II

Security Zones

Buildings and homes should be looked at from the approach of visualization of security zones. View the building, your apartment or home as a series of squares or rectangles that have **different security problems and goals.** High-rise buildings, especially apartment buildings, tend to be complex. Before dividing into security zones, the types of security and the types of people and things to be secured must be assessed. Types of people and/ or equipment which are particularly vulnerable to attack should be placed in a separate and secure area especially away from entrances and exits. If security is to be at a high level, there should be at least one security guard on each building floor and controlled access to each floor.

Defensible Space

Within the zone concept is that of defensible space, that is, proper **physical layouts** can allow those in a building to **control behavior of the potential terrorist.**

If the people in a building can recognize one another, they will be alert to who may not belong in the building. In the case of office buildings, this can be accomplished with photo I.D. badges. In apartment buildings of considerable size, a directory of residents with their photos can be used. Digitized pass cards for electric locks are extremely useful to minimize intrusion into any part of a building. Patio and garden areas should not be public areas. These areas should be private. Again security zones are needed. The use of walls and fences can accomplish this.

Zones of Transition

The concept of zones of transition rests in the idea that a series of security zones should exist which place the terrorist on notice that he is entering through a number of zones of security. This can be done with simple architectural structures such as walls, setbacks, steps, low level plantings (less than 5 feet in height), large exterior windows and more obvious items such as signs and guard stations. Exterior closed-circuit television, which is quite obvious can be extremely effective for discouraging terrorists from entering both office and apartment buildings. The costs of such apparatus are surprisingly reasonable today: an apartment building might be done for less than one dollar per tenant per month for the first year with the system being amortized over that one year. Large apartment complexes should use perimeter fencing, walls or a combination thereof. Ideally, lobby and elevator areas should be observable from the front of the building. This latter setup can prevent personal attacks in lobbies and elevators since the terrorist may be easily observed.

WINDOWS FROM DWELLING
SURVEY DEFINED REALM

PLANTER AND PLANTS BUFFER DWELLING
FROM COLLECTIVE GROUNDS

RECESSED ALCOVE DEFINES
ENTRY TO UNIT

LANDING AND CHANGE IN LEVEL
HELP DEFINE THE UNIT

LIGHTING AND COLUMNS
DEFINE ENTRY PORTAL

LOW WALL DEFINES COLLECTIVE
SEMIPRIVATE AREA

SMALL SETBACK CREATES A SIDEWALK ZONE
BELONGING TO THE RESIDENTIAL CLUSTER

CHANGE IN SURFACE TEXTURE CREATES
FIRST ELEMENT OF TRANSITION

PLANTING BUFFERS UNIT
FROM SIDEWALK

Zones of Transition

LL

The Security Command Center

No matter how large or small the building, **some type of security command center is necessary.** It may be a simple desk in the front entrance area. Where electronic security equipment is used, a central command center should incorporate the alarm and CCTV systems. The center should also incorporate immediate transmission features, e.g., direct lines to the police, the ability to notify each office or apartment of an immediate hazard or threat. Thus the command center represents an integration of all security systems at one location. Obviously, the most sophisticated command center is one of little value if it lacks a human being to monitor the systems.

Visitors to buildings should be issued temporary **passes which immediately identify them as visitors.** For even tighter control, passes may be additionally color controlled to indicate which floor the visitor shall be allowed access to. A visitor pass with the visitor's picture on it is best.

Passes for Workmen

Too often little attention is paid to what appear to be workmen in a building. They often wander into all areas of a building with total immunity. **Workman should be issued special passes which by size and color identify them a workmen.**

Employee/Resident Pass Systems

The pass system is only effective to the point, which it is enforced. **Passes of employees or residents should have expiration dates** so that the guards can know which employees/residents are no longer should be in the building.

In the system where guards hand out and collect employee passes at the end of the day, it will be known who still remains in the building.

Hospital - I.D. Badges

Because hospitals are such large and confusing institutions, it is very important that all hospital personnel wear standardized identification badges. Since it is very easy for a terrorist to slip on another person's labcoat, i.d. badge and all, **identification badges should have pictures of the assigned employee.** Such a system will allow patients and visitors to recognize hospital staff and will also facilitate such recognition by the security staff.

Apartments

The ideal apartment setup has closed circuit television, electronic front door access and a front door security guard.

Since many terrorists are there to infect mailboxes, mailboxes should be in clear lobby view. It is sometimes helpful to place lounge chairs and furniture in the lobby in clear view of the entrance; the terrorist will fear that tenants will come down to sit in the lobby. Basement recreation, laundry and canteen facilities are extremely poor security zones since they afford the terrorist his own private room for terror. In both apartment and office buildings, entry doors should have large glass or see through plastic portions. Stairwell doors should be keyed so that only exit is possible. Tenants of the building can have keys that will open the doors onto floors and restrooms. Exits will be only at ground level for the non-tenant.

Elevators

Each elevator should have a communication system that will connect the passenger with either the security desk and/ or the management. Closed circuit television is a must for the large office or apartment building served by elevators, i.e., each elevator should be monitored. Many terrorists are adept at disabling elevators between floors. Control panels must be secured so that they cannot be removed and the elevator disabled. Emergency stop buttons should have alarms. If the terrorist can't open the control panel, he can't disable the emergency stop alarm. A high security elevator is one which requires either a key or digital card to access the elevator; a further security measure is also to have the elevator doors open from the inside with such a key or card.

Windows

Windows that are at ground level should not have lower ledges, which are less than six feet from the ground. Nothing should be near the windows which can aid the terrorist in getting up to and through the window: ladders, hedges, walls, parking cars, garbage cans, utility pipes, fire escapes, etc. Fire escape ladders should be at least 10 feet off the ground until activated.

Delivery and Shipping Bays

Delivery and shipping bays should be located where they can be observed by office personnel in the building, as well as, interior workers. Warehouse offices should be positioned so that the bay areas are easily observable even under casual circumstances.

Security Layouts - Building Exteriors

Trees and bushes are natural hiding places for terrorists, especially where the vegetation is placed close to building entrances/exits and pathways leading to and from a building. Where employees have inside views of outside areas, the views should not be blocked by vegetation. The central mission is to **keep all terrorist activity within full view** of those outside the building and within maximum view of inside employees.

Buildings which may be subject to terrorist attack should be in full view from all roads and pathways near the building; additionally concrete and/or steel barriers should surround the building to stop crash-ramming of the building.

Building Entrance-Exit Systems

A security outpost at a single entrance-exit system is -the ideal arrangement for almost any public or private building. If a security post is not present, a reception area should be in full view of the entrance. If neither a security post nor reception desk is used, the building management office should be at the front entrance and should have full view of the entrance; extensive upper window walling would be necessary for such a management office. Often one encounters office buildings where there is no security post or reception area and the management office is above street level. By no stretch of the imagination is the management in the latter case providing any building security.

Emergency exits are too often positioned in remote places. These exits should be in clear view from both the outside and inside so as to prevent their use for both terrorist entrance and exit. Such emergency doors should have alarm systems. Emergency exits should be painted bright-contrasting colors in reference to the building and should be clearly marked from both the inside and outside as emergency exits only. Many emergency areas open onto grass sod areas; the latter will make anyone using the exit look out of place. If discharge is onto a concrete area, that area should be marked in a contrasting manner to the main entrance area.

Retail Stores and Shops

Terrorists prefer shops and stores whose interiors are not easily visible from the street. Shelves and **displays should not be higher than 5 feet. Aisles should**

be perpendicular to the check out/cashier area so that the store personnel can see who is in each aisle. The check out/ cashier stands should be in clear view from the street and should be raised behind the counter area, at least 6 inches above the sales floor level. These simple steps will go a long way in preventing terrorist acts.

Time-Security Ratings

Even the most secure building will be prone to some level of terrorist activity. A key factor is how long it would take to penetrate the security zone. The longer it takes, the greater the chance the terrorist will be caught.

Layers of Security Zones

The more layers of security zones the terrorist has to break through, the greater the probability he will be caught. Like the layers of an onion, layers of security zones are simple:

Layer One: Building Perimeter
Layer Two: Parking Lots, Courtyards and Patios
Layer Three: Doors and Windows (outer)
Layer Four: Foyer and Hallways

Layer Five: Stairwells and Elevators
Layer Six: Inner Hallways
Layer Seven: Inner Door and Window Systems

Style Before Security

The design and layout of many buildings, especially office buildings and motel-hotel buildings, are planned only in terms of the visual effects the building will yield. Little or no attention is directed at the security factors, which will be involved in the operation. A good security expert should be able to speak to the security layout of the building.

Perimeter Fences and Walls

A security wall or fence should be at least 6 feet in height. Where security is to be at a maximum, various climbing or scaling barriers can be placed atop the fence or wall, e.g., barbed wire, electric wires, spikes, etc.

Fences and walls should be of an open or see through type. Closed walls and fences provide protective cover for the terrorist. If chain link fences are used,

UU

the openings in the mesh should not be greater than two (2) inches, so that toes cannot fit into the mesh spaces. The bottom of the chain should be fastened and embedded into concrete to prevent burrowing under the fence.

Glass

Most buildings have glass windows and doors, which have annealed glass. Annealed glass is specially heated and rolled. Unfortunately, annealed glass is not very plastic, that is, it offers hardly any resistance to impact; thus it breaks easily. The terrorist will cover the annealed glass with tape, break the glass which sticks to the tape and remove the broken glass which has not fallen to the ground. Virtually no noise of broken glass will be heard. Terrorist resistant glass does exist. There is also security glass which is bullet-proof; there are also several types of bullet-proof plastics available. In terms of safety where such bullet or break-in proof glasses or plastics are used, special quick release window and door catches are also available. The professional terrorist can be kept out only with plastic types of security glazing. Break-in resistant glass must be at least one-half inch thick while break-in resistant plastic should be at least one inch thick. Where terrorist attacks may occur, all glazing should be plastic coated to prevent injuries from

VV

flying glass. Plastic coatings also aid in deterring break-ins.

Tamper Resistant Nuts, Screws and Bolts

A screwdriver is often the only tool needed to enter a building. It is very important that tamper resistant nuts, bolts and screws be used. Such hardware cannot be unscrewed without virtually destroying the hardware. There are special screw and bolt heads, which take special tools to unfasten them.

Computer Monitored Security Systems

Where only one guard is assigned to monitor various electronic intrusion detection devices, the task will be great, too great, for one security operator. One guard can monitor such a system only when it is computerized. Remote microprocessors located in the alarms and detection systems can be in continuous communication with the central desk computer. These systems can be designed up so that if the guard does not respond to security situations, the computer will automatically contact either the police or other security personnel.

Electronic Door Locks

Electronic door lock systems, sometimes commercially referred to as Cypher Locks, are readily available. A correct number sequence must be punched in or entry will not be permitted. These codes also can be changed periodically.

Metal Window Barriers

Metal grates, grilles and bars are a most effective means of keeping terrorists out of buildings. Such devices must have quick release mechanisms for emergencies such as fires.

Any metal window protections should minimally be 1/8 inch in diameter. Openings should not exceed two inches. Window bards should not be greater than 5 inches from each other.